The Law School Admission Council (LSAC) is a nonprofit corporation that provides unique, state-of-the-art admission products and services to ease the admission process for law schools and their applicants worldwide. More than 200 law schools in the United States, Canada, and Australia are members of the Council and benefit from LSAC's services.

ISBN-13: 978-0-9846360-1-3
ISBN-10: 0-9846360-1-3

TABLE OF CONTENTS

The Law School Admission Test is a half-day standardized test required for admission to all ABA-approved law schools, most Canadian law schools, and many other law schools. It consists of five 35-minute sections of multiple-choice questions. Four of the five sections contribute to the test taker's score. These sections include one Reading Comprehension section, one Analytical Reasoning section, and two Logical Reasoning sections. The unscored section, commonly referred to as the variable section, typically is used to pretest new test questions or to preequate new test forms. The placement of this section in the LSAT will vary. A 35-minute writing sample is administered at the end of the test. The writing sample is not scored by LSAC, but copies are sent to all law schools to which you apply. The score scale for the LSAT is 120 to 180.

The LSAT is designed to measure skills considered essential for success in law school: the reading and comprehension of complex texts with accuracy and insight; the organization and management of information and the ability to draw reasonable inferences from it; the ability to think critically; and the analysis and evaluation of the reasoning and arguments of others.

The LSAT provides a standard measure of acquired reading and verbal reasoning skills that law schools can use as one of several factors in assessing applicants.

For up-to-date information about LSAC's services, go to our website, LSAC.org.

SCORING

Your LSAT score is based on the number of questions you answer correctly (the raw score). There is no deduction for incorrect answers, and all questions count equally. In other words, there is no penalty for guessing.

Test Score Accuracy—Reliability and Standard Error of Measurement

Candidates perform at different levels on different occasions for reasons quite unrelated to the characteristics of a test itself. The accuracy of test scores is best described by the use of two related statistical terms: reliability and standard error of measurement.

Reliability is a measure of how consistently a test measures the skills being assessed. The higher the reliability coefficient for a test, the more certain we can be that test takers would get very similar scores if they took the test again.

LSAC reports an internal consistency measure of reliability for every test form. Reliability can vary from 0.00 to 1.00, and a test with no measurement error would have a reliability coefficient of 1.00 (never attained in practice). Reliability

coefficients for past LSAT forms have ranged from .90 to .95, indicating a high degree of consistency for these tests. LSAC expects the reliability of the LSAT to continue to fall within the same range.

LSAC also reports the amount of measurement error associated with each test form, a concept known as the standard error of measurement (SEM). The SEM, which is usually about 2.6 points, indicates how close a test taker's observed score is likely to be to his or her true score. True scores are theoretical scores that would be obtained from perfectly reliable tests with no measurement error—scores never known in practice.

Score bands, or ranges of scores that contain a test taker's true score a certain percentage of the time, can be derived using the SEM. LSAT score bands are constructed by adding and subtracting the (rounded) SEM to and from an actual LSAT score (e.g., the LSAT score, plus or minus 3 points). Scores near 120 or 180 have asymmetrical bands. Score bands constructed in this manner will contain an individual's true score approximately 68 percent of the time.

Measurement error also must be taken into account when comparing LSAT scores of two test takers. It is likely that small differences in scores are due to measurement error rather than to meaningful differences in ability. The standard error of score differences provides some guidance as to the importance of differences between two scores. The standard error of score differences is approximately 1.4 times larger than the standard error of measurement for the individual scores.

Thus, a test score should be regarded as a useful but approximate measure of a test taker's abilities as measured by the test, not as an exact determination of his or her abilities. LSAC encourages law schools to examine the range of scores within the interval that probably contains the test taker's true score (e.g., the test taker's score band) rather than solely interpret the reported score alone.

Adjustments for Variation in Test Difficulty

All test forms of the LSAT reported on the same score scale are designed to measure the same abilities, but one test form may be slightly easier or more difficult than another. The scores from different test forms are made comparable through a statistical procedure known as equating. As a result of equating, a given scaled score earned on different test forms reflects the same level of ability.

Research on the LSAT

Summaries of LSAT validity studies and other LSAT research can be found in member law school libraries and at LSAC.org.

To Inquire About Test Questions

If you find what you believe to be an error or ambiguity in a test question that affects your response to the question, contact LSAC by e-mail: LSATTS@LSAC.org, or write to Law School Admission Council, Test Development Group, PO Box 40, Newtown, PA 18940-0040.

HOW THIS PREPTEST DIFFERS FROM AN ACTUAL LSAT

This PrepTest is made up of the scored sections and writing sample from the actual disclosed LSAT administered in June 2011. However, it does not contain the extra, variable section that is used to pretest new test items of one of the three multiple-choice question types. The three multiple-choice question types may be in a different order in an actual LSAT than in this PrepTest. This is because the order of these question types is intentionally varied for each administration of the test.

THE THREE LSAT MULTIPLE-CHOICE QUESTION TYPES

The multiple-choice questions that make up most of the LSAT reflect a broad range of academic disciplines and are intended to give no advantage to candidates from a particular academic background.

The five sections of the test contain three different question types. The following material presents a general discussion of the nature of each question type and some strategies that can be used in answering them.

Analytical Reasoning Questions

Analytical Reasoning questions are designed to assess the ability to consider a group of facts and rules, and, given those facts and rules, determine what could or must be true. The specific scenarios associated with these questions are usually unrelated to law, since they are intended to be accessible to a wide range of test takers. However, the skills tested parallel those involved in determining what could or must be the case given a set of regulations, the terms of a contract, or the facts of a legal case in relation to the law. In Analytical Reasoning questions, you are asked to reason deductively from a set of statements and rules or principles that describe relationships among persons, things, or events.

Analytical Reasoning questions appear in sets, with each set based on a single passage. The passage used for each set of questions describes common ordering relationships or grouping relationships, or a combination of both types of relationships. Examples include scheduling employees for work shifts, assigning instructors to class sections,

ordering tasks according to priority, and distributing grants for projects.

Analytical Reasoning questions test a range of deductive reasoning skills. These include:

- Comprehending the basic structure of a set of relationships by determining a complete solution to the problem posed (for example, an acceptable seating arrangement of all six diplomats around a table)

- Reasoning with conditional ("if-then") statements and recognizing logically equivalent formulations of such statements

- Inferring what could be true or must be true from given facts and rules

- Inferring what could be true or must be true from given facts and rules together with new information in the form of an additional or substitute fact or rule

- Recognizing when two statements are logically equivalent in context by identifying a condition or rule that could replace one of the original conditions while still resulting in the same possible outcomes

Analytical Reasoning questions reflect the kinds of detailed analyses of relationships and sets of constraints that a law student must perform in legal problem solving. For example, an Analytical Reasoning passage might describe six diplomats being seated around a table, following certain rules of protocol as to who can sit where. You, the test taker, must answer questions about the logical implications of given and new information. For example, you may be asked who can sit between diplomats X and Y, or who cannot sit next to X if W sits next to Y. Similarly, if you were a student in law school, you might be asked to analyze a scenario involving a set of particular circumstances and a set of governing rules in the form of constitutional provisions, statutes, administrative codes, or prior rulings that have been upheld. You might then be asked to determine the legal options in the scenario: what is required given the scenario, what is permissible given the scenario, and what is prohibited given the scenario. Or you might be asked to develop a "theory" for the case: when faced with an incomplete set of facts about the case, you must fill in the picture based on what is implied by the facts that are known. The problem could be elaborated by the addition of new information or hypotheticals.

No formal training in logic is required to answer these questions correctly. Analytical Reasoning questions are intended to be answered using knowledge, skills, and reasoning ability generally expected of college students and graduates.

Suggested Approach

Some people may prefer to answer first those questions about a passage that seem less difficult and then those that seem more difficult. In general, it is best to finish one passage before starting on another, because much time can be lost in returning to a passage and reestablishing familiarity with its relationships. However, if you are having great difficulty on one particular set of questions and are spending too much time on them, it may be to your advantage to skip that set of questions and go on to the next passage, returning to the problematic set of questions after you have finished the other questions in the section.

Do not assume that because the conditions for a set of questions look long or complicated, the questions based on those conditions will be especially difficult.

Read the passage carefully. Careful reading and analysis are necessary to determine the exact nature of the relationships involved in an Analytical Reasoning passage. Some relationships are fixed (for example, P and R must always work on the same project). Other relationships are variable (for example, Q must be assigned to either team 1 or team 3). Some relationships that are not stated explicitly in the conditions are implied by and can be deduced from those that are stated (for example, if one condition about paintings in a display specifies that Painting K must be to the left of Painting Y, and another specifies that Painting W must be to the left of Painting K, then it can be deduced that Painting W must be to the left of Painting Y).

In reading the conditions, do not introduce unwarranted assumptions. For instance, in a set of questions establishing relationships of height and weight among the members of a team, do not assume that a person who is taller than another person must weigh more than that person. As another example, suppose a set involves ordering and a question in the set asks what must be true if both X and Y must be earlier than Z; in this case, do not assume that X must be earlier than Y merely because X is mentioned before Y. All the information needed to answer each question is provided in the passage and the question itself.

The conditions are designed to be as clear as possible. Do not interpret the conditions as if they were intended to trick you. For example, if a question asks how many people could be eligible to serve on a committee, consider only those people named in the passage unless directed otherwise. When in doubt, read the conditions in their most obvious sense. Remember, however, that the language in the conditions is intended to be read for precise meaning. It is essential to pay particular attention to words that describe or limit relationships, such as "only," "exactly," "never," "always," "must be," "cannot be," and the like.

The result of this careful reading will be a clear picture of the structure of the relationships involved, including the kinds of relationships permitted, the participants in the relationships, and the range of possible actions or attributes for these participants.

Keep in mind question independence. Each question should be considered separately from the other questions in its set. No information, except what is given in the original conditions, should be carried over from one question to another.

In some cases a question will simply ask for conclusions to be drawn from the conditions as originally given. Some questions may, however, add information to the original conditions or temporarily suspend or replace one of the original conditions for the purpose of that question only. For example, if Question 1 adds the supposition "if P is sitting at table 2 ...," this supposition should NOT be carried over to any other question in the set.

Consider highlighting text and using diagrams. Many people find it useful to underline key points in the passage and in each question. In addition, it may prove very helpful to draw a diagram to assist you in finding the solution to the problem.

In preparing for the test, you may wish to experiment with different types of diagrams. For a scheduling problem, a simple calendar-like diagram may be helpful. For a grouping problem, an array of labeled columns or rows may be useful.

Even though most people find diagrams to be very helpful, some people seldom use them, and for some individual questions no one will need a diagram. There is by no means universal agreement on which kind of diagram is best for which problem or in which cases a diagram is most useful. Do not be concerned if a particular problem in the test seems to be best approached without the use of a diagram.

Logical Reasoning Questions

Arguments are a fundamental part of the law, and analyzing arguments is a key element of legal analysis. Training in the law builds on a foundation of basic reasoning skills. Law students must draw on the skills of analyzing, evaluating, constructing, and refuting arguments. They need to be able to identify what information is relevant to an issue or argument and what impact further evidence might have. They need to be able to reconcile opposing positions and use arguments to persuade others.

Logical Reasoning questions evaluate the ability to analyze, critically evaluate, and complete arguments as they occur in ordinary language. The questions are based on short arguments drawn from a wide variety of sources, including newspapers, general interest magazines, scholarly publications, advertisements, and informal discourse. These arguments mirror legal reasoning in the types of arguments presented and in their complexity, though few of the arguments actually have law as a subject matter.

Each Logical Reasoning question requires you to read and comprehend a short passage, then answer one question (or, rarely, two questions) about it. The questions are designed to assess a wide range of skills involved in thinking critically, with an emphasis on skills that are central to legal reasoning.

These skills include:

- Recognizing the parts of an argument and their relationships

- Recognizing similarities and differences between patterns of reasoning

- Drawing well-supported conclusions

- Reasoning by analogy

- Recognizing misunderstandings or points of disagreement

- Determining how additional evidence affects an argument

- Detecting assumptions made by particular arguments

- Identifying and applying principles or rules

- Identifying flaws in arguments

- Identifying explanations

The questions do not presuppose specialized knowledge of logical terminology. For example, you will not be expected to know the meaning of specialized terms such as "ad hominem" or "syllogism." On the other hand, you will be expected to understand and critique the reasoning contained in arguments. This requires that you possess a university-level understanding of widely used concepts such as argument, premise, assumption, and conclusion.

Suggested Approach

Read each question carefully. Make sure that you understand the meaning of each part of the question. Make sure that you understand the meaning of each answer choice and the ways in which it may or may not relate to the question posed.

Do not pick a response simply because it is a true statement. Although true, it may not answer the question posed.

Answer each question on the basis of the information that is given, even if you do not agree with it. Work within the context provided by the passage. LSAT questions do not involve any tricks or hidden meanings.

Reading Comprehension Questions

Both law school and the practice of law revolve around extensive reading of highly varied, dense, argumentative, and expository texts (for example, cases, codes, contracts, briefs, decisions, evidence). This reading must be exacting, distinguishing precisely what is said from what is not said. It involves comparison, analysis, synthesis, and application (for example, of principles and rules). It involves drawing appropriate inferences and applying ideas and arguments to new contexts. Law school reading also requires the ability to grasp unfamiliar subject matter and the ability to penetrate difficult and challenging material.

The purpose of LSAT Reading Comprehension questions is to measure the ability to read, with understanding and insight, examples of lengthy and complex materials similar to those commonly encountered in law school. The Reading Comprehension section of the LSAT contains four sets of reading questions, each set consisting of a selection of reading material followed by five to eight questions. The reading selection in three of the four sets consists of a single reading passage; the other set contains two related shorter passages. Sets with two passages are a variant of Reading Comprehension called Comparative Reading, which was introduced in June 2007.

Comparative Reading questions concern the relationships between the two passages, such as those of generalization/instance, principle/application, or point/counterpoint. Law school work often requires reading two or more texts in conjunction with each other and understanding their relationships. For example, a law student may read a trial court decision together with an appellate court decision that overturns it, or identify the fact pattern from a hypothetical suit together with the potentially controlling case law.

Reading selections for LSAT Reading Comprehension questions are drawn from a wide range of subjects in the humanities, the social sciences, the biological and physical sciences, and areas related to the law. Generally, the selections are densely written, use high-level vocabulary, and contain sophisticated argument or complex rhetorical structure (for example, multiple points of view). Reading Comprehension questions require you to read carefully and accurately, to determine the relationships among the various parts of the reading selection, and to draw reasonable inferences from the material in the selection. The questions may ask about the following characteristics of a passage or pair of passages:

- The main idea or primary purpose

- Information that is explicitly stated

- Information or ideas that can be inferred

- Information or ideas that can be inferred

- The meaning or purpose of words or phrases as used in context

- The organization or structure

- The application of information in the selection to a new context

- Principles that function in the selection

- Analogies to claims or arguments in the selection

- An author's attitude as revealed in the tone of a passage or the language used

- The impact of new information on claims or arguments in the selection

Suggested Approach

Since reading selections are drawn from many different disciplines and sources, you should not be discouraged if you encounter material with which you are not familiar. It is important to remember that questions are to be answered exclusively on the basis of the information provided in the selection. There is no particular knowledge that you are expected to bring to the test, and you should not make inferences based on any prior knowledge of a subject that you may have. You may, however, wish to defer working on a set of questions that seems particularly difficult or unfamiliar until after you have dealt with sets you find easier.

Strategies. One question that often arises in connection with Reading Comprehension has to do with the most effective and efficient order in which to read the selections and questions. Possible approaches include:

- reading the selection very closely and then answering the questions;

- reading the questions first, reading the selection closely, and then returning to the questions; or

- skimming the selection and questions very quickly, then rereading the selection closely and answering the questions.

Test takers are different, and the best strategy for one might not be the best strategy for another. In preparing for the test, therefore, you might want to experiment with the different strategies and decide what works most effectively for you.

Remember that your strategy must be effective under timed conditions. For this reason, the first strategy—reading the selection very closely and then answering

the questions—may be the most effective for you. Nonetheless, if you believe that one of the other strategies might be more effective for you, you should try it out and assess your performance using it.

Reading the selection. Whatever strategy you choose, you should give the passage or pair of passages at least one careful reading before answering the questions. Try to distinguish main ideas from supporting ideas, and opinions or attitudes from factual, objective information. Note transitions from one idea to the next and identify the relationships among the different ideas or parts of a passage, or between the two passages in Comparative Reading sets. Consider how and why an author makes points and draws conclusions. Be sensitive to implications of what the passages say.

You may find it helpful to mark key parts of passages. For example, you might underline main ideas or important arguments, and you might circle transitional words—"although," "nevertheless," "correspondingly," and the like—that will help you map the structure of a passage. Also, you might note descriptive words that will help you identify an author's attitude toward a particular idea or person.

Answering the Questions

- Always read all the answer choices before selecting the best answer. The best answer choice is the one that most accurately and completely answers the question being posed.

- Respond to the specific question being asked. Do not pick an answer choice simply because it is a true statement. For example, picking a true statement might yield an incorrect answer to a question in which you are asked to identify an author's position on an issue, since you are not being asked to evaluate the truth of the author's position but only to correctly identify what that position is.

- Answer the questions only on the basis of the information provided in the selection. Your own views, interpretations, or opinions, and those you have heard from others, may sometimes conflict with those expressed in a reading selection; however, you are expected to work within the context provided by the reading selection. You should not expect to agree with everything you encounter in Reading Comprehension passages.

THE WRITING SAMPLE

On the day of the test, you will be asked to write one sample essay. LSAC does not score the writing sample, but copies are sent to all law schools to which you apply. According to a 2006 LSAC survey of 157 United States and to respond to writing sample prompts and frivolous responses have been used by law schools as grounds for rejection of applications for admission.

In developing and implementing the writing sample portion of the LSAT, LSAC has operated on the following premises: First, law schools and the legal profession value highly the ability to communicate effectively in writing. Second, it is important to encourage potential law students to develop effective writing skills. Third, a sample of an applicant's writing, produced under controlled conditions, is a potentially useful indication of that person's writing ability. Fourth, the writing sample can serve as an independent check on other writing submitted by applicants as part of the admission process. Finally, writing samples may be useful for diagnostic purposes related to improving a candidate's writing.

The writing prompt presents a decision problem. You are asked to make a choice between two positions or courses of action. Both of the choices are defensible, and you are given criteria and facts on which to base your decision. There is no "right" or "wrong" position to take on the topic, so the quality of each test taker's response is a function not of which choice is made, but of how well or poorly the choice is supported and how well or poorly the other choice is criticized.

The LSAT writing prompt was designed and validated by legal education professionals. Since it involves writing based on fact sets and criteria, the writing sample gives applicants the opportunity to demonstrate the type of argumentative writing that is required in law school, although the topics are usually nonlegal.

You will have 35 minutes in which to plan and write an essay on the topic you receive. Read the topic and the accompanying directions carefully. You will probably find it best to spend a few minutes considering the topic and organizing your thoughts before you begin writing. In your essay, be sure to develop your ideas fully, leaving time, if possible, to review what you have written. Do not write on a topic other than the one specified. Writing on a topic of your own choice is not acceptable.

No special knowledge is required or expected for this writing exercise. Law schools are interested in the reasoning, clarity, organization, language usage, and writing mechanics displayed in your essay. How well you write is more important than how much you write. Confine your essay to the blocked, lined area on the front and back of the separate Writing Sample Response Sheet. Only that area will be reproduced for law schools. Be sure that your writing is legible.

TAKING THE PREPTEST UNDER SIMULATED LSAT CONDITIONS

One important way to prepare for the LSAT is to simulate the day of the test by taking a practice test under actual time constraints. Taking a practice test under timed conditions helps you to estimate the amount of time you can afford to spend on each question in a section and to determine the question types on which you may need additional practice.

Since the LSAT is a timed test, it is important to use your allotted time wisely. During the test, you may work only on the section designated by the test supervisor. You cannot devote extra time to a difficult section and make up that time on a section you find easier. In pacing yourself, and checking your answers, you should think of each section of the test as a separate minitest.

Be sure that you answer every question on the test. When you do not know the correct answer to a question, first eliminate the responses that you know are incorrect, then make your best guess among the remaining choices. Do not be afraid to guess as there is no penalty for incorrect answers.

When you take a practice test, abide by all the requirements specified in the directions and keep strictly within the specified time limits. Work without a rest period. When you take an actual test, you will have only a short break—usually 10–15 minutes—after SECTION III.

When taken under conditions as much like actual testing conditions as possible, a practice test provides very useful preparation for taking the LSAT.

Official directions for the four multiple-choice sections and the writing sample are included in this PrepTest so that you can approximate actual testing conditions as you practice.

To take the test:

- Set a timer for 35 minutes. Answer all the questions in SECTION I of this PrepTest. Stop working on that section when the 35 minutes have elapsed.

- Repeat, allowing yourself 35 minutes each for sections II, III, and IV.

- Set the timer again for 35 minutes, then prepare your response to the writing sample topic at the end of this PrepTest.

- Refer to "Computing Your Score" for the PrepTest for instruction on evaluating your performance. An answer key is provided for that purpose.

The practice test that follows consists of four sections corresponding to the four scored sections of the June 2011 LSAT. Also reprinted is the June 2011 unscored writing sample topic.

General Directions for the LSAT Answer Sheet

The actual testing time for this portion of the test will be 2 hours 55 minutes. There are five sections, each with a time limit of 35 minutes. The supervisor will tell you when to begin and end each section. If you finish a section before time is called, you may check your work on that section only; do not turn to any other section of the test book and do not work on any other section either in the test book or on the answer sheet.

There are several different types of questions on the test, and each question type has its own directions. Be sure you understand the directions for each question type before attempting to answer any questions in that section.

Not everyone will finish all the questions in the time allowed. Do not hurry, but work steadily and as quickly as you can without sacrificing accuracy. You are advised to use your time effectively. If a question seems too difficult, go on to the next one and return to the difficult question after completing the section. MARK THE BEST ANSWER YOU CAN FOR EVERY QUESTION. NO DEDUCTIONS WILL BE MADE FOR WRONG ANSWERS. YOUR SCORE WILL BE BASED ONLY ON THE NUMBER OF QUESTIONS YOU ANSWER CORRECTLY.

ALL YOUR ANSWERS MUST BE MARKED ON THE ANSWER SHEET. Answer spaces for each question are lettered to correspond with the letters of the potential answers to each question in the test book. After you have decided which of the answers is correct, blacken the corresponding space on the answer sheet. BE SURE THAT EACH MARK IS BLACK AND COMPLETELY FILLS THE ANSWER SPACE. Give only one answer to each question. If you change an answer, be sure that all previous marks are erased completely. Since the answer sheet is machine scored, incomplete erasures may be interpreted as intended answers. ANSWERS RECORDED IN THE TEST BOOK WILL NOT BE SCORED.

There may be more question numbers on this answer sheet than there are questions in a section. Do not be concerned, but be certain that the section and number of the question you are answering matches the answer sheet section and question number. Additional answer spaces in any answer sheet section should be left blank. Begin your next section in the number one answer space for that section.

LSAC takes various steps to ensure that answer sheets are returned from test centers in a timely manner for processing. In the unlikely event that an answer sheet is not received, LSAC will permit the examinee either to retest at no additional fee or to receive a refund of his or her LSAT fee. THESE REMEDIES ARE THE ONLY REMEDIES AVAILABLE IN THE UNLIKELY EVENT THAT AN ANSWER SHEET IS NOT RECEIVED BY LSAC.

Score Cancellation

Complete this section only if you are absolutely certain you want to cancel your score. A CANCELLATION REQUEST CANNOT BE RESCINDED. IF YOU ARE AT ALL UNCERTAIN, YOU SHOULD NOT COMPLETE THIS SECTION.

To cancel your score from this administration, you must:

A. fill in both ovals here ..... ○ ○
 AND

B. read the following statement. Then sign your name and enter the date. **YOUR SIGNATURE ALONE IS NOT SUFFICIENT FOR SCORE CANCELLATION. BOTH OVALS ABOVE MUST BE FILLED IN FOR SCANNING EQUIPMENT TO RECOGNIZE YOUR REQUEST FOR SCORE CANCELLATION.**

I certify that I wish to cancel my test score from this administration. I understand that my request is irreversible and that my score will not be sent to me or to the law schools to which I apply.

_____
Sign your name in full

_____
Date

FOR LSAC USE ONLY ●

HOW DID YOU PREPARE FOR THE LSAT?
(Select all that apply.)

Responses to this item are voluntary and will be used for statistical research purposes only.

○ By studying the free sample questions available on LSAC's website.
○ By taking the free sample LSAT available on LSAC's website.
○ By working through official LSAT *PrepTests, ItemWise,* and/or other LSAC test prep products.
○ By using LSAT prep books or software not published by LSAC.
○ By attending a commercial test preparation or coaching course.
○ By attending a test preparation or coaching course offered through an undergraduate institution.
○ Self study.
○ Other preparation.
○ No preparation.

CERTIFYING STATEMENT

Please write the following statement. Sign and date.

I certify that I am the examinee whose name appears on this answer sheet and that I am here to take the LSAT for the sole purpose of being considered for admission to law school. I further certify that I will neither assist nor receive assistance from any other candidate, and I agree not to copy, retain, or transmit examination questions in any form or discuss them with any other person.

_____
_____
_____
_____
_____
_____
_____
_____

SIGNATURE: _____   TODAY'S DATE: ___/___/___
                                                        MONTH DAY YEAR

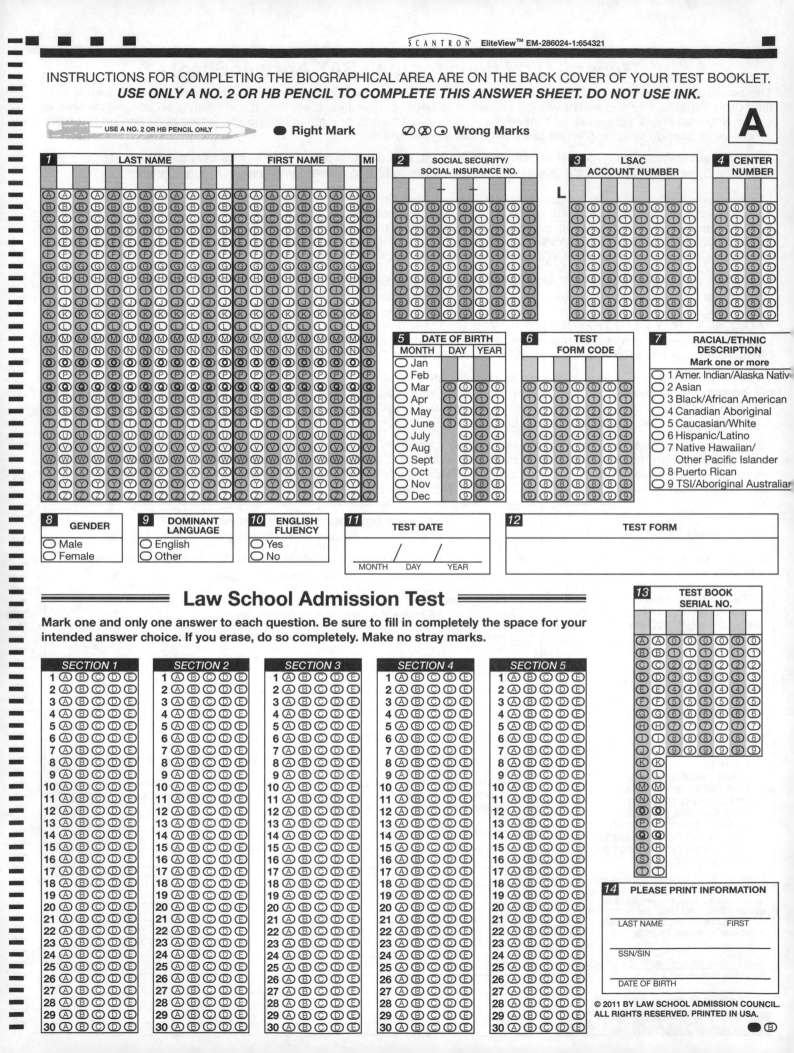

THE PREPTEST

SECTION I

Time—35 minutes

25 Questions

Directions: The questions in this section are based on the reasoning contained in brief statements or passages. For some questions, more than one of the choices could conceivably answer the question. However, you are to choose the best answer; that is, the response that most accurately and completely answers the question. You should not make assumptions that are by commonsense standards implausible, superfluous, or incompatible with the passage. After you have chosen the best answer, blacken the corresponding space on your answer sheet.

1. Backyard gardeners who want to increase the yields of their potato plants should try growing stinging nettles alongside the plants, since stinging nettles attract insects that kill a wide array of insect pests that damage potato plants. It is true that stinging nettles also attract aphids, and that many species of aphids are harmful to potato plants, but that fact in no way contradicts this recommendation, because _____.

Which one of the following most logically completes the argument?

(A) stinging nettles require little care and thus are easy to cultivate

(B) some types of aphids are attracted to stinging nettle plants but do not damage them

(C) the types of aphids that stinging nettles attract do not damage potato plants

(D) insect pests typically cause less damage to potato plants than other harmful organisms do

(E) most aphid species that are harmful to potato plants cause greater harm to other edible food plants

2. Jocko, a chimpanzee, was once given a large bunch of bananas by a zookeeper after the more dominant members of the chimpanzee's troop had wandered off. In his excitement, Jocko uttered some loud "food barks." The other chimpanzees returned and took the bananas away. The next day, Jocko was again found alone and was given a single banana. This time, however, he kept silent. The zookeeper concluded that Jocko's silence was a stratagem to keep the other chimpanzees from his food.

Which one of the following, if true, most seriously calls into question the zookeeper's conclusion?

(A) Chimpanzees utter food barks only when their favorite foods are available.

(B) Chimpanzees utter food barks only when they encounter a sizable quantity of food.

(C) Chimpanzees frequently take food from other chimpanzees merely to assert dominance.

(D) Even when they are alone, chimpanzees often make noises that appear to be signals to other chimpanzees.

(E) Bananas are a food for which all of the chimpanzees at the zoo show a decided preference.

3. A recent survey quizzed journalism students about the sorts of stories they themselves wished to read. A significant majority said they wanted to see stories dealing with serious governmental and political issues and had little tolerance for the present popularity of stories covering lifestyle trends and celebrity gossip. This indicates that today's trends in publishing are based on false assumptions about the interests of the public.

Which one of the following most accurately describes a flaw in the argument's reasoning?

(A) It takes what is more likely to be the effect of a phenomenon to be its cause.

(B) It regards the production of an effect as incontrovertible evidence of an intention to produce that effect.

(C) It relies on the opinions of a group unlikely to be representative of the group at issue in the conclusion.

(D) It employs language that unfairly represents those who are likely to reject the argument's conclusion.

(E) It treats a hypothesis as fact even though it is admittedly unsupported.

GO ON TO THE NEXT PAGE.

4. Electric bug zappers, which work by attracting insects to light, are a very effective means of ridding an area of flying insects. Despite this, most pest control experts now advise against their use, recommending instead such remedies as insect-eating birds or insecticide sprays.

Which one of the following, if true, most helps to account for the pest control experts' recommendation?

(A)   Insect-eating birds will take up residence in any insect-rich area if they are provided with nesting boxes, food, and water.

(B)   Bug zappers are less effective against mosquitoes, which are among the more harmful insects, than they are against other harmful insects.

(C)   Bug zappers use more electricity but provide less light than do most standard outdoor light sources.

(D)   Bug zappers kill many more beneficial insects and fewer harmful insects than do insect-eating birds and insecticide sprays.

(E)   Developers of certain new insecticide sprays claim that their products contain no chemicals that are harmful to humans, birds, or pets.

5. Gardener: The design of Japanese gardens should display harmony with nature. Hence, rocks chosen for placement in such gardens should vary widely in appearance, since rocks found in nature also vary widely in appearance.

The gardener's argument depends on assuming which one of the following?

(A)   The selection of rocks for placement in a Japanese garden should reflect every key value embodied in the design of Japanese gardens.

(B)   In the selection of rocks for Japanese gardens, imitation of nature helps to achieve harmony with nature.

(C)   The only criterion for selecting rocks for placement in a Japanese garden is the expression of harmony with nature.

(D)   Expressing harmony with nature and being natural are the same thing.

(E)   Each component of a genuine Japanese garden is varied.

6. Small experimental vacuum tubes can operate in heat that makes semiconductor components fail. Any component whose resistance to heat is greater than that of semiconductors would be preferable for use in digital circuits, but only if that component were also comparable to semiconductors in all other significant respects, such as maximum current capacity. However, vacuum tubes' maximum current capacity is presently not comparable to that of semiconductors.

If the statements above are true, which one of the following must also be true?

(A)   Vacuum tubes are not now preferable to semiconductors for use in digital circuits.

(B)   Once vacuum tubes and semiconductors have comparable maximum current capacity, vacuum tubes will be used in some digital circuits.

(C)   The only reason that vacuum tubes are not now used in digital circuits is that vacuum tubes' maximum current capacity is too low.

(D)   Semiconductors will always be preferable to vacuum tubes for use in many applications other than digital circuits.

(E)   Resistance to heat is the only advantage that vacuum tubes have over semiconductors.

7. The cause of the epidemic that devastated Athens in 430 B.C. can finally be identified. Accounts of the epidemic mention the hiccups experienced by many victims, a symptom of no known disease except that caused by the recently discovered Ebola virus. Moreover, other symptoms of the disease caused by the Ebola virus are mentioned in the accounts of the Athenian epidemic.

Each of the following, if true, weakens the argument EXCEPT:

(A)   Victims of the Ebola virus experience many symptoms that do not appear in any of the accounts of the Athenian epidemic.

(B)   Not all of those who are victims of the Ebola virus are afflicted with hiccups.

(C)   The Ebola virus's host animals did not live in Athens at the time of the Athenian epidemic.

(D)   The Ebola virus is much more contagious than the disease that caused the Athenian epidemic was reported to have been.

(E)   The epidemics known to have been caused by the Ebola virus are usually shorter-lived than was the Athenian epidemic.

GO ON TO THE NEXT PAGE.

8. Letter to the editor: Your article was unjustified in criticizing environmentalists for claiming that more wolves on Vancouver Island are killed by hunters than are born each year. You stated that this claim was disproven by recent studies that indicate that the total number of wolves on Vancouver Island has remained roughly constant for 20 years. But you failed to account for the fact that, fearing the extinction of this wolf population, environmentalists have been introducing new wolves into the Vancouver Island wolf population for 20 years.

Which one of the following most accurately expresses the conclusion of the argument in the letter to the editor?

(A) Environmentalists have been successfully maintaining the wolf population on Vancouver Island for 20 years.

(B) As many wolves on Vancouver Island are killed by hunters as are born each year.

(C) The population of wolves on Vancouver Island should be maintained by either reducing the number killed by hunters each year or introducing new wolves into the population.

(D) The recent studies indicating that the total number of wolves on Vancouver Island has remained roughly constant for 20 years were flawed.

(E) The stability in the size of the Vancouver Island wolf population does not warrant the article's criticism of the environmentalists' claim.

9. Computer scientist: For several decades, the number of transistors on new computer microchips, and hence the microchips' computing speed, has doubled about every 18 months. However, from the mid-1990s into the next decade, each such doubling in a microchip's computing speed was accompanied by a doubling in the cost of producing that microchip.

Which one of the following can be properly inferred from the computer scientist's statements?

(A) The only effective way to double the computing speed of computer microchips is to increase the number of transistors per microchip.

(B) From the mid-1990s into the next decade, there was little if any increase in the retail cost of computers as a result of the increased number of transistors on microchips.

(C) For the last several decades, computer engineers have focused on increasing the computing speed of computer microchips without making any attempt to control the cost of producing them.

(D) From the mid-1990s into the next decade, a doubling in the cost of fabricating new computer microchips accompanied each doubling in the number of transistors on those microchips.

(E) It is unlikely that engineers will ever be able to increase the computing speed of microchips without also increasing the cost of producing them.

GO ON TO THE NEXT PAGE.

10. Ms. Sandstrom's newspaper column describing a strange natural phenomenon on the Mendels' farm led many people to trespass on and extensively damage their property. Thus, Ms. Sandstrom should pay for this damage if, as the Mendels claim, she could have reasonably expected that the column would lead people to damage the Mendels' farm.

The argument's conclusion can be properly inferred if which one of the following is assumed?

(A) One should pay for any damage that one's action leads other people to cause if one could have reasonably expected that the action would lead other people to cause damage.

(B) One should pay for damage that one's action leads other people to cause only if, prior to the action, one expected that the action would lead other people to cause that damage.

(C) It is unlikely that the people who trespassed on and caused the damage to the Mendels' property would themselves pay for the damage they caused.

(D) Ms. Sandstrom knew that her column could incite trespassing that could result in damage to the Mendels' farm.

(E) The Mendels believe that Ms. Sandstrom is able to form reasonable expectations about the consequences of her actions.

11. Meyer was found by his employer to have committed scientific fraud by falsifying data. The University of Williamstown, from which Meyer held a PhD, validated this finding and subsequently investigated whether he had falsified data in his doctoral thesis, finding no evidence that he had. But the university decided to revoke Meyer's PhD anyway.

Which one of the following university policies most justifies the decision to revoke Meyer's PhD?

(A) Anyone who holds a PhD from the University of Williamstown and is found to have committed academic fraud in the course of pursuing that PhD will have the PhD revoked.

(B) No PhD program at the University of Williamstown will admit any applicant who has been determined to have committed any sort of academic fraud.

(C) Any University of Williamstown student who is found to have submitted falsified data as academic work will be dismissed from the university.

(D) Anyone who holds a PhD from the University of Williamstown and is found to have committed scientific fraud will have the PhD revoked.

(E) The University of Williamstown will not hire anyone who is under investigation for scientific fraud.

12. Aerobics instructor: Compared to many forms of exercise, kickboxing aerobics is highly risky. Overextending when kicking often leads to hip, knee, or lower-back injuries. Such overextension is very likely to occur when beginners try to match the high kicks of more skilled practitioners.

Which one of the following is most strongly supported by the aerobics instructor's statements?

(A) Skilled practitioners of kickboxing aerobics are unlikely to experience injuries from overextending while kicking.

(B) To reduce the risk of injuries, beginners at kickboxing aerobics should avoid trying to match the high kicks of more skilled practitioners.

(C) Beginners at kickboxing aerobics will not experience injuries if they avoid trying to match the high kicks of more skilled practitioners.

(D) Kickboxing aerobics is more risky than forms of aerobic exercise that do not involve high kicks.

(E) Most beginners at kickboxing aerobics experience injuries from trying to match the high kicks of more skilled practitioners.

13. A large company has been convicted of engaging in monopolistic practices. The penalty imposed on the company will probably have little if any effect on its behavior. Still, the trial was worthwhile, since it provided useful information about the company's practices. After all, this information has emboldened the company's direct competitors, alerted potential rivals, and forced the company to restrain its unfair behavior toward customers and competitors.

Which one of the following most accurately expresses the overall conclusion drawn in the argument?

(A) Even if the company had not been convicted of engaging in monopolistic practices, the trial probably would have had some effect on the company's behavior.

(B) The light shed on the company's practices by the trial has emboldened its competitors, alerted potential rivals, and forced the company to restrain its unfair behavior.

(C) The penalty imposed on the company will likely have little or no effect on its behavior.

(D) The company's trial on charges of engaging in monopolistic practices was worthwhile.

(E) The penalty imposed on the company in the trial should have been larger.

GO ON TO THE NEXT PAGE.

14. Waller: If there were really such a thing as extrasensory perception, it would generally be accepted by the public since anyone with extrasensory powers would be able to convince the general public of its existence by clearly demonstrating those powers. Indeed, anyone who was recognized to have such powers would achieve wealth and renown.

Chin: It's impossible to demonstrate anything to the satisfaction of all skeptics. So long as the cultural elite remains closed-minded to the possibility of extrasensory perception, the popular media reports, and thus public opinion, will always be biased in favor of such skeptics.

Waller's and Chin's statements commit them to disagreeing on whether

(A) extrasensory perception is a real phenomenon
(B) extrasensory perception, if it were a real phenomenon, could be demonstrated to the satisfaction of all skeptics
(C) skeptics about extrasensory perception have a weak case
(D) the failure of the general public to believe in extrasensory perception is good evidence against its existence
(E) the general public believes that extrasensory perception is a real phenomenon

15. Counselor: Hagerle sincerely apologized to the physician for lying to her. So Hagerle owes me a sincere apology as well, because Hagerle told the same lie to both of us.

Which one of the following principles, if valid, most helps to justify the counselor's reasoning?

(A) It is good to apologize for having done something wrong to a person if one is capable of doing so sincerely.
(B) If someone tells the same lie to two different people, then neither of those lied to is owed an apology unless both are.
(C) Someone is owed a sincere apology for having been lied to by a person if someone else has already received a sincere apology for the same lie from that same person.
(D) If one is capable of sincerely apologizing to someone for lying to them, then one owes that person such an apology.
(E) A person should not apologize to someone for telling a lie unless he or she can sincerely apologize to all others to whom the lie was told.

16. A survey of address changes filed with post offices and driver's license bureaus over the last ten years has established that households moving out of the city of Weston outnumbered households moving into the city two to one. Therefore, we can expect that next year's census, which counts all residents regardless of age, will show that the population of Weston has declined since the last census ten years ago.

Which one of the following, if true, most helps strengthen the argument?

(A) Within the past decade many people both moved into the city and also moved out of it.
(B) Over the past century any census of Weston showing a population loss was followed ten years later by a census showing a population gain.
(C) Many people moving into Weston failed to notify either the post office or the driver's license bureau that they had moved to the city.
(D) Most adults moving out of Weston were parents who had children living with them, whereas most adults remaining in or moving into the city were older people who lived alone.
(E) Most people moving out of Weston were young adults who were hoping to begin a career elsewhere, whereas most adults remaining in or moving into the city had long-standing jobs in the city.

17. Psychologist: People tend to make certain cognitive errors when they predict how a given event would affect their future happiness. But people should not necessarily try to rid themselves of this tendency. After all, in a visual context, lines that are actually parallel often appear to people as if they converge. If a surgeon offered to restructure your eyes and visual cortex so that parallel lines would no longer ever appear to converge, it would not be reasonable to take the surgeon up on the offer.

The psychologist's argument does which one of the following?

(A) attempts to refute a claim that a particular event is inevitable by establishing the possibility of an alternative event
(B) attempts to undermine a theory by calling into question an assumption on which the theory is based
(C) argues that an action might not be appropriate by suggesting that a corresponding action in an analogous situation is not appropriate
(D) argues that two situations are similar by establishing that the same action would be reasonable in each situation
(E) attempts to establish a generalization and then uses that generalization to argue against a particular action

GO ON TO THE NEXT PAGE.

18. Principle: Even if an art auction house identifies the descriptions in its catalog as opinions, it is guilty of misrepresentation if such a description is a deliberate attempt to mislead bidders.

Application: Although Healy's, an art auction house, states that all descriptions in its catalog are opinions, Healy's was guilty of misrepresentation when its catalog described a vase as dating from the mid-eighteenth century when it was actually a modern reproduction.

Which one of the following, if true, most justifies the above application of the principle?

(A) An authentic work of art from the mid-eighteenth century will usually sell for at least ten times more than a modern reproduction of a similar work from that period.

(B) Although pottery that is similar to the vase is currently extremely popular among art collectors, none of the collectors who are knowledgeable about such pottery were willing to bid on the vase.

(C) The stated policy of Healy's is to describe works in its catalogs only in terms of their readily perceptible qualities and not to include any information about their age.

(D) Some Healy's staff members believe that the auction house's catalog should not contain any descriptions that have not been certified to be true by independent experts.

(E) Without consulting anyone with expertise in authenticating vases, Healy's described the vase as dating from the mid-eighteenth century merely in order to increase its auction price.

19. Anthropologist: It was formerly believed that prehistoric *Homo sapiens* ancestors of contemporary humans interbred with Neanderthals, but DNA testing of a Neanderthal's remains indicates that this is not the case. The DNA of contemporary humans is significantly different from that of the Neanderthal.

Which one of the following is an assumption required by the anthropologist's argument?

(A) At least some Neanderthals lived at the same time and in the same places as prehistoric *Homo sapiens* ancestors of contemporary humans.

(B) DNA testing of remains is significantly less reliable than DNA testing of samples from living species.

(C) The DNA of prehistoric *Homo sapiens* ancestors of contemporary humans was not significantly more similar to that of Neanderthals than is the DNA of contemporary humans.

(D) Neanderthals and prehistoric *Homo sapiens* ancestors of contemporary humans were completely isolated from each other geographically.

(E) Any similarity in the DNA of two species must be the result of interbreeding.

20. Council member: The profits of downtown businesses will increase if more consumers live in the downtown area, and a decrease in the cost of living in the downtown area will guarantee that the number of consumers living there will increase. However, the profits of downtown businesses will not increase unless downtown traffic congestion decreases.

If all the council member's statements are true, which one of the following must be true?

(A) If downtown traffic congestion decreases, the number of consumers living in the downtown area will increase.

(B) If the cost of living in the downtown area decreases, the profits of downtown businesses will increase.

(C) If downtown traffic congestion decreases, the cost of living in the downtown area will increase.

(D) If downtown traffic congestion decreases, the cost of living in the downtown area will decrease.

(E) If the profits of downtown businesses increase, the number of consumers living in the downtown area will increase.

GO ON TO THE NEXT PAGE.

21. On the Discount Phoneline, any domestic long-distance call starting between 9 A.M. and 5 P.M. costs 15 cents a minute, and any other domestic long-distance call costs 10 cents a minute. So any domestic long-distance call on the Discount Phoneline that does not cost 10 cents a minute costs 15 cents a minute.

The pattern of reasoning in which one of the following arguments is most similar to that in the argument above?

(A) If a university class involves extensive lab work, the class will be conducted in a laboratory; otherwise, it will be conducted in a normal classroom. Thus, if a university class does not involve extensive lab work, it will not be conducted in a laboratory.

(B) If a university class involves extensive lab work, the class will be conducted in a laboratory; otherwise, it will be conducted in a normal classroom. Thus, if a university class is not conducted in a normal classroom, it will involve extensive lab work.

(C) If a university class involves extensive lab work, the class will be conducted in a laboratory; otherwise, it will be conducted in a normal classroom. Thus, if a university class is conducted in a normal classroom, it will not be conducted in a laboratory.

(D) If a university class involves extensive lab work, the class will be conducted in a laboratory; otherwise, it will be conducted in a normal classroom. Thus, if a university class involves extensive lab work, it will not be conducted in a normal classroom.

(E) If a university class involves extensive lab work, the class will be conducted in a laboratory; otherwise, it will be conducted in a normal classroom. Thus, if a university class is not conducted in a normal classroom, it will be conducted in a laboratory.

22. One child pushed another child from behind, injuring the second child. The first child clearly understands the difference between right and wrong, so what was done was wrong if it was intended to injure the second child.

Which one of the following principles, if valid, most helps to justify the reasoning in the argument?

(A) An action that is intended to harm another person is wrong only if the person who performed the action understands the difference between right and wrong.

(B) It is wrong for a person who understands the difference between right and wrong to intentionally harm another person.

(C) Any act that is wrong is done with the intention of causing harm.

(D) An act that harms another person is wrong if the person who did it understands the difference between right and wrong and did not think about whether the act would injure the other person.

(E) A person who does not understand the difference between right and wrong does not bear any responsibility for harming another person.

23. Researcher: Each subject in this experiment owns one car, and was asked to estimate what proportion of all automobiles registered in the nation are the same make as the subject's car. The estimate of nearly every subject has been significantly higher than the actual national statistic for the make of that subject's car. I hypothesize that certain makes of car are more common in some regions of the nation than in other regions; obviously, that would lead many people to overestimate how common their make of car is nationally. That is precisely the result found in this experiment, so certain makes of car must indeed be more common in some areas of the nation than in others.

Which one of the following most accurately expresses a reasoning flaw in the researcher's argument?

(A) The argument fails to estimate the likelihood that most subjects in the experiment did not know the actual statistics about how common their make of car is nationwide.

(B) The argument treats a result that supports a hypothesis as a result that proves a hypothesis.

(C) The argument fails to take into account the possibility that the subject pool may come from a wide variety of geographical regions.

(D) The argument attempts to draw its main conclusion from a set of premises that are mutually contradictory.

(E) The argument applies a statistical generalization to a particular case to which it was not intended to apply.

GO ON TO THE NEXT PAGE.

24. In university towns, police issue far more parking citations during the school year than they do during the times when the students are out of town. Therefore, we know that most parking citations in university towns are issued to students.

Which one of the following is most similar in its flawed reasoning to the flawed reasoning in the argument above?

(A) We know that children buy most of the snacks at cinemas, because popcorn sales increase as the proportion of child moviegoers to adult moviegoers increases.

(B) We know that this houseplant gets more of the sunlight from the window, because it is greener than that houseplant.

(C) We know that most people who go to a university are studious because most of those people study while they attend the university.

(D) We know that consumers buy more fruit during the summer than they buy during the winter, because there are far more varieties of fruit available in the summer than in the winter.

(E) We know that most of the snacks parents buy go to other people's children, because when other people's children come to visit, parents give out more snacks than usual.

25. Counselor: Those who believe that criticism should be gentle rather than harsh should consider the following: change requires a motive, and criticism that is unpleasant provides a motive. Since harsh criticism is unpleasant, harsh criticism provides a motive. Therefore, only harsh criticism will cause the person criticized to change.

The reasoning in the counselor's argument is most vulnerable to criticism on the grounds that the argument

(A) infers that something that is sufficient to provide a motive is necessary to provide a motive

(B) fails to address the possibility that in some cases the primary goal of criticism is something other than bringing about change in the person being criticized

(C) takes for granted that everyone who is motivated to change will change

(D) confuses a motive for doing something with a motive for avoiding something

(E) takes the refutation of an argument to be sufficient to show that the argument's conclusion is false

STOP

IF YOU FINISH BEFORE TIME IS CALLED, YOU MAY CHECK YOUR WORK ON THIS SECTION ONLY.
DO NOT WORK ON ANY OTHER SECTION IN THE TEST.

SECTION II
Time—35 minutes
23 Questions

Directions: Each group of questions in this section is based on a set of conditions. In answering some of the questions, it may be useful to draw a rough diagram. Choose the response that most accurately and completely answers each question and blacken the corresponding space on your answer sheet.

Questions 1–5

Each of seven candidates for the position of judge—Hamadi, Jefferson, Kurtz, Li, McDonnell, Ortiz, and Perkins—will be appointed to an open position on one of two courts—the appellate court or the trial court. There are three open positions on the appellate court and six open positions on the trial court, but not all of them will be filled at this time. The judicial appointments will conform to the following conditions:
   Li must be appointed to the appellate court.
   Kurtz must be appointed to the trial court.
   Hamadi cannot be appointed to the same court as Perkins.

1. Which one of the following is an acceptable set of appointments of candidates to courts?

   (A)   appellate: Hamadi, Ortiz
        trial: Jefferson, Kurtz, Li, McDonnell, Perkins
   (B)   appellate: Hamadi, Li, Perkins
        trial: Jefferson, Kurtz, McDonnell, Ortiz
   (C)   appellate: Kurtz, Li, Perkins
        trial: Hamadi, Jefferson, McDonnell, Ortiz
   (D)   appellate: Li, McDonnell, Ortiz
        trial: Hamadi, Jefferson, Kurtz, Perkins
   (E)   appellate: Li, Perkins
        trial: Hamadi, Jefferson, Kurtz, McDonnell, Ortiz

2. Which one of the following CANNOT be true?

   (A)   Hamadi and McDonnell are both appointed to the appellate court.
   (B)   McDonnell and Ortiz are both appointed to the appellate court.
   (C)   Ortiz and Perkins are both appointed to the appellate court.
   (D)   Hamadi and Jefferson are both appointed to the trial court.
   (E)   Ortiz and Perkins are both appointed to the trial court.

3. Which one of the following CANNOT be true?

   (A)   Jefferson and McDonnell are both appointed to the appellate court.
   (B)   Jefferson and McDonnell are both appointed to the trial court.
   (C)   McDonnell and Ortiz are both appointed to the trial court.
   (D)   McDonnell and Perkins are both appointed to the appellate court.
   (E)   McDonnell and Perkins are both appointed to the trial court.

4. If Ortiz is appointed to the appellate court, which one of the following must be true?

   (A)   Hamadi is appointed to the appellate court.
   (B)   Jefferson is appointed to the appellate court.
   (C)   Jefferson is appointed to the trial court.
   (D)   Perkins is appointed to the appellate court.
   (E)   Perkins is appointed to the trial court.

5. Which one of the following, if substituted for the condition that Hamadi cannot be appointed to the same court as Perkins, would have the same effect on the appointments of the seven candidates?

   (A)   Hamadi and Perkins cannot both be appointed to the appellate court.
   (B)   If Hamadi is not appointed to the trial court, then Perkins must be.
   (C)   If Perkins is appointed to the same court as Jefferson, then Hamadi cannot be.
   (D)   If Hamadi is appointed to the same court as Li, then Perkins must be appointed to the same court as Kurtz.
   (E)   No three of Hamadi, Kurtz, Li, and Perkins can be appointed to the same court as each other.

GO ON TO THE NEXT PAGE.

Questions 6–10

Exactly six members of a skydiving team—Larue, Ohba, Pei, Treviño, Weiss, and Zacny—each dive exactly once, one at a time, from a plane, consistent with the following conditions:

Treviño dives from the plane at some time before Weiss does.

Larue dives from the plane either first or last.

Neither Weiss nor Zacny dives from the plane last.

Pei dives from the plane at some time after either Ohba or Larue but not both.

6. Which one of the following could be an accurate list of the members in the order in which they dive from the plane, from first to last?

(A) Larue, Treviño, Ohba, Zacny, Pei, Weiss
(B) Larue, Treviño, Pei, Zacny, Weiss, Ohba
(C) Weiss, Ohba, Treviño, Zacny, Pei, Larue
(D) Treviño, Weiss, Pei, Ohba, Zacny, Larue
(E) Treviño, Weiss, Zacny, Larue, Pei, Ohba

7. Which one of the following must be true?

(A) At least two of the members dive from the plane after Larue.
(B) At least two of the members dive from the plane after Ohba.
(C) At least two of the members dive from the plane after Pei.
(D) At least two of the members dive from the plane after Treviño.
(E) At least two of the members dive from the plane after Weiss.

8. If Larue dives from the plane last, then each of the following could be true EXCEPT:

(A) Treviño dives from the plane fourth.
(B) Weiss dives from the plane fourth.
(C) Ohba dives from the plane fifth.
(D) Pei dives from the plane fifth.
(E) Zacny dives from the plane fifth.

9. If Zacny dives from the plane immediately after Weiss, then which one of the following must be false?

(A) Larue dives from the plane first.
(B) Treviño dives from the plane third.
(C) Zacny dives from the plane third.
(D) Pei dives from the plane fourth.
(E) Zacny dives from the plane fourth.

10. If Treviño dives from the plane immediately after Larue, then each of the following could be true EXCEPT:

(A) Ohba dives from the plane third.
(B) Weiss dives from the plane third.
(C) Zacny dives from the plane third.
(D) Pei dives from the plane fourth.
(E) Weiss dives from the plane fourth.

GO ON TO THE NEXT PAGE.

Questions 11–17

A company's six vehicles—a hatchback, a limousine, a pickup, a roadster, a sedan, and a van—are serviced during a certain week—Monday through Saturday—one vehicle per day. The following conditions must apply:

At least one of the vehicles is serviced later in the week than the hatchback.

The roadster is serviced later in the week than the van and earlier in the week than the hatchback.

Either the pickup and the van are serviced on consecutive days, or the pickup and the sedan are serviced on consecutive days, but not both.

The sedan is serviced earlier in the week than the pickup or earlier in the week than the limousine, but not both.

11. Which one of the following could be the order in which the vehicles are serviced, from Monday through Saturday?

(A) the hatchback, the pickup, the sedan, the limousine, the van, the roadster
(B) the pickup, the sedan, the van, the roadster, the hatchback, the limousine
(C) the pickup, the van, the sedan, the roadster, the limousine, the hatchback
(D) the van, the roadster, the pickup, the hatchback, the sedan, the limousine
(E) the van, the sedan, the pickup, the roadster, the hatchback, the limousine

12. Which one of the following CANNOT be the vehicle serviced on Thursday?

(A) the hatchback
(B) the limousine
(C) the pickup
(D) the sedan
(E) the van

13. If neither the pickup nor the limousine is serviced on Monday, then which one of the following must be true?

(A) The hatchback and the limousine are serviced on consecutive days.
(B) The hatchback and the sedan are serviced on consecutive days.
(C) The van is serviced on Monday.
(D) The limousine is serviced on Saturday.
(E) The pickup is serviced on Saturday.

14. If the limousine is not serviced on Saturday, then each of the following could be true EXCEPT:

(A) The limousine is serviced on Monday.
(B) The roadster is serviced on Tuesday.
(C) The hatchback is serviced on Wednesday.
(D) The roadster is serviced on Wednesday.
(E) The sedan is serviced on Wednesday.

15. If the sedan is serviced earlier in the week than the pickup, then which one of the following could be true?

(A) The limousine is serviced on Wednesday.
(B) The sedan is serviced on Wednesday.
(C) The van is serviced on Wednesday.
(D) The hatchback is serviced on Friday.
(E) The limousine is serviced on Saturday.

16. If the limousine is serviced on Saturday, then which one of the following must be true?

(A) The pickup is serviced earlier in the week than the roadster.
(B) The pickup is serviced earlier in the week than the sedan.
(C) The sedan is serviced earlier in the week than the roadster.
(D) The hatchback and the limousine are serviced on consecutive days.
(E) The roadster and the hatchback are serviced on consecutive days.

17. Which one of the following could be the list of the vehicles serviced on Tuesday, Wednesday, and Friday, listed in that order?

(A) the pickup, the hatchback, the limousine
(B) the pickup, the roadster, the hatchback
(C) the sedan, the limousine, the hatchback
(D) the van, the limousine, the hatchback
(E) the van, the roadster, the limousine

GO ON TO THE NEXT PAGE.

Questions 18–23

A street entertainer has six boxes stacked one on top of the other and numbered consecutively 1 through 6, from the lowest box up to the highest. Each box contains a single ball, and each ball is one of three colors—green, red, or white. Onlookers are to guess the color of each ball in each box, given that the following conditions hold:

There are more red balls than white balls.

There is a box containing a green ball that is lower in the stack than any box that contains a red ball.

There is a white ball in a box that is immediately below a box that contains a green ball.

18. If there are exactly two white balls, then which one of the following boxes could contain a green ball?

   (A) box 1
   (B) box 3
   (C) box 4
   (D) box 5
   (E) box 6

19. If there are green balls in boxes 5 and 6, then which one of the following could be true?

   (A) There are red balls in boxes 1 and 4.
   (B) There are red balls in boxes 2 and 4.
   (C) There is a white ball in box 1.
   (D) There is a white ball in box 2.
   (E) There is a white ball in box 3.

20. The ball in which one of the following boxes must be the same color as at least one of the other balls?

   (A) box 2
   (B) box 3
   (C) box 4
   (D) box 5
   (E) box 6

21. Which one of the following must be true?

   (A) There is a green ball in a box that is lower than box 4.
   (B) There is a green ball in a box that is higher than box 4.
   (C) There is a red ball in a box that is lower than box 4.
   (D) There is a red ball in a box that is higher than box 4.
   (E) There is a white ball in a box that is lower than box 4.

22. If there are red balls in boxes 2 and 3, then which one of the following could be true?

   (A) There is a red ball in box 1.
   (B) There is a white ball in box 1.
   (C) There is a green ball in box 4.
   (D) There is a red ball in box 5.
   (E) There is a white ball in box 6.

23. If boxes 2, 3, and 4 all contain balls that are the same color as each other, then which one of the following must be true?

   (A) Exactly two of the boxes contain a green ball.
   (B) Exactly three of the boxes contain a green ball.
   (C) Exactly three of the boxes contain a red ball.
   (D) Exactly one of the boxes contains a white ball.
   (E) Exactly two of the boxes contain a white ball.

S T O P

IF YOU FINISH BEFORE TIME IS CALLED, YOU MAY CHECK YOUR WORK ON THIS SECTION ONLY.
DO NOT WORK ON ANY OTHER SECTION IN THE TEST.

SECTION III

Time—35 minutes

26 Questions

Directions: The questions in this section are based on the reasoning contained in brief statements or passages. For some questions, more than one of the choices could conceivably answer the question. However, you are to choose the best answer; that is, the response that most accurately and completely answers the question. You should not make assumptions that are by commonsense standards implausible, superfluous, or incompatible with the passage. After you have chosen the best answer, blacken the corresponding space on your answer sheet.

1. Commentator: In last week's wreck involving one of Acme Engines' older locomotives, the engineer lost control of the train when his knee accidentally struck a fuel shut-down switch. Acme claims it is not liable because it never realized that the knee-level switches were a safety hazard. When asked why it relocated knee-level switches in its newer locomotives, Acme said engineers had complained that they were simply inconvenient. However, it is unlikely that Acme would have spent the $500,000 it took to relocate switches in the newer locomotives merely because of inconvenience. Thus, Acme Engines should be held liable for last week's wreck.

The point that Acme Engines spent $500,000 relocating knee-level switches in its newer locomotives is offered in the commentator's argument as

(A) proof that the engineer is not at all responsible for the train wreck
(B) a reason for believing that the wreck would have occurred even if Acme Engines had remodeled their older locomotives
(C) an explanation of why the train wreck occurred
(D) evidence that knee-level switches are not in fact hazardous
(E) an indication that Acme Engines had been aware of the potential dangers of knee-level switches before the wreck occurred

2. Artist: Almost everyone in this country really wants to be an artist even though they may have to work other jobs to pay the rent. After all, just about everyone I know hopes to someday be able to make a living as a painter, musician, or poet even if they currently work as dishwashers or discount store clerks.

The reasoning in the artist's argument is flawed in that the argument

(A) contains a premise that presupposes the truth of the conclusion
(B) presumes that what is true of each person in a country is also true of the country's population as a whole
(C) defends a view solely on the grounds that the view is widely held
(D) bases its conclusion on a sample that is unlikely to accurately represent people in the country as a whole
(E) fails to make a needed distinction between wanting to be an artist and making a living as an artist

3. The qwerty keyboard became the standard keyboard with the invention of the typewriter and remains the standard for typing devices today. If an alternative known as the Dvorak keyboard were today's standard, typists would type significantly faster. Nevertheless, it is not practical to switch to the Dvorak keyboard because the cost to society of switching, in terms of time, money, and frustration, would be greater than the benefits that would be ultimately gained from faster typing.

The example above best illustrates which one of the following propositions?

(A) Often it is not worthwhile to move to a process that improves speed if it comes at the expense of accuracy.
(B) People usually settle on a standard because that standard is more efficient than any alternatives.
(C) People often remain with an entrenched standard rather than move to a more efficient alternative simply because they dislike change.
(D) The emotional cost associated with change is a factor that sometimes outweighs financial considerations.
(E) The fact that a standard is already in wide use can be a crucial factor in making it a more practical choice than an alternative.

GO ON TO THE NEXT PAGE.

4. Sam: Mountain lions, a protected species, are preying on bighorn sheep, another protected species. We must let nature take its course and hope the bighorns survive.

   Meli: Nonsense. We must do what we can to ensure the survival of the bighorn, even if that means limiting the mountain lion population.

   Which one of the following is a point of disagreement between Meli and Sam?

   (A) Humans should not intervene to protect bighorn sheep from mountain lions.
   (B) The preservation of a species as a whole is more important than the loss of a few individuals.
   (C) The preservation of a predatory species is easier to ensure than the preservation of the species preyed upon.
   (D) Any measures to limit the mountain lion population would likely push the species to extinction.
   (E) If the population of mountain lions is not limited, the bighorn sheep species will not survive.

5. Parent: Pushing very young children into rigorous study in an effort to make our nation more competitive does more harm than good. Curricula for these young students must address their special developmental needs, and while rigorous work in secondary school makes sense, the same approach in the early years of primary school produces only short-term gains and may cause young children to burn out on schoolwork. Using very young students as pawns in the race to make the nation economically competitive is unfair and may ultimately work against us.

   Which one of the following can be inferred from the parent's statements?

   (A) For our nation to be competitive, our secondary school curriculum must include more rigorous study than it now does.
   (B) The developmental needs of secondary school students are not now being addressed in our high schools.
   (C) Our country can be competitive only if the developmental needs of all our students can be met.
   (D) A curriculum of rigorous study does not adequately address the developmental needs of primary school students.
   (E) Unless our nation encourages more rigorous study in the early years of primary school, we cannot be economically competitive.

6. A transit company's bus drivers are evaluated by supervisors riding with each driver. Drivers complain that this affects their performance, but because the supervisor's presence affects every driver's performance, those drivers performing best with a supervisor aboard will likely also be the best drivers under normal conditions.

   Which one of the following is an assumption on which the argument depends?

   (A) There is no effective way of evaluating the bus drivers' performance without having supervisors ride with them.
   (B) The supervisors are excellent judges of a bus driver's performance.
   (C) For most bus drivers, the presence of a supervisor makes their performance slightly worse than it otherwise would be.
   (D) The bus drivers are each affected in roughly the same way and to the same extent by the presence of the supervisor.
   (E) The bus drivers themselves are able to deliver accurate assessments of their driving performance.

7. Economic growth accelerates business demand for the development of new technologies. Businesses supplying these new technologies are relatively few, while those wishing to buy them are many. Yet an acceleration of technological change can cause suppliers as well as buyers of new technologies to fail.

   Which one of the following is most strongly supported by the information above?

   (A) Businesses supplying new technologies are more likely to prosper in times of accelerated technological change than other businesses.
   (B) Businesses that supply new technologies may not always benefit from economic growth.
   (C) The development of new technologies may accelerate economic growth in general.
   (D) Businesses that adopt new technologies are most likely to prosper in a period of general economic growth.
   (E) Economic growth increases business failures.

GO ON TO THE NEXT PAGE.

8. Energy analyst: During this record-breaking heat wave, air conditioner use has overloaded the region's electrical power grid, resulting in frequent power blackouts throughout the region. For this reason, residents have been asked to cut back voluntarily on air conditioner use in their homes. But even if this request is heeded, blackouts will probably occur unless the heat wave abates.

Which one of the following, if true, most helps to resolve the apparent discrepancy in the information above?

(A) Air-conditioning is not the only significant drain on the electrical system in the area.

(B) Most air-conditioning in the region is used to cool businesses and factories.

(C) Most air-conditioning systems could be made more energy efficient by implementing simple design modifications.

(D) Residents of the region are not likely to reduce their air conditioner use voluntarily during particularly hot weather.

(E) The heat wave is expected to abate in the near future.

9. Long-term and short-term relaxation training are two common forms of treatment for individuals experiencing problematic levels of anxiety. Yet studies show that on average, regardless of which form of treatment one receives, symptoms of anxiety decrease to a normal level within the short-term-training time period. Thus, for most people the generally more expensive long-term training is unwarranted.

Which one of the following, if true, most weakens the argument?

(A) A decrease in symptoms of anxiety often occurs even with no treatment or intervention by a mental health professional.

(B) Short-term relaxation training conducted by a more experienced practitioner can be more expensive than long-term training conducted by a less experienced practitioner.

(C) Recipients of long-term training are much less likely than recipients of short-term training to have recurrences of problematic levels of anxiety.

(D) The fact that an individual thinks that a treatment will reduce his or her anxiety tends, in and of itself, to reduce the individual's anxiety.

(E) Short-term relaxation training involves the teaching of a wider variety of anxiety-combating relaxation techniques than does long-term training.

10. Editorial: Many critics of consumerism insist that advertising persuades people that they need certain consumer goods when they merely desire them. However, this accusation rests on a fuzzy distinction, that between wants and needs. In life, it is often impossible to determine whether something is merely desirable or whether it is essential to one's happiness.

Which one of the following most accurately expresses the conclusion drawn in the editorial's argument?

(A) The claim that advertising persuades people that they need things that they merely want rests on a fuzzy distinction.

(B) Many critics of consumerism insist that advertising attempts to blur people's ability to distinguish between wants and needs.

(C) There is nothing wrong with advertising that tries to persuade people that they need certain consumer goods.

(D) Many critics of consumerism fail to realize that certain things are essential to human happiness.

(E) Critics of consumerism often use fuzzy distinctions to support their claims.

11. People who browse the web for medical information often cannot discriminate between scientifically valid information and quackery. Much of the quackery is particularly appealing to readers with no medical background because it is usually written more clearly than scientific papers. Thus, people who rely on the web when attempting to diagnose their medical conditions are likely to do themselves more harm than good.

Which one of the following is an assumption the argument requires?

(A) People who browse the web for medical information typically do so in an attempt to diagnose their medical conditions.

(B) People who attempt to diagnose their medical conditions are likely to do themselves more harm than good unless they rely exclusively on scientifically valid information.

(C) People who have sufficient medical knowledge to discriminate between scientifically valid information and quackery will do themselves no harm if they rely on the web when attempting to diagnose their medical conditions.

(D) Many people who browse the web assume that information is not scientifically valid unless it is clearly written.

(E) People attempting to diagnose their medical conditions will do themselves more harm than good only if they rely on quackery instead of scientifically valid information.

GO ON TO THE NEXT PAGE.

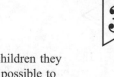

12. When adults toss balls to very young children they generally try to toss them as slowly as possible to compensate for the children's developing coordination. But recent studies show that despite their developing coordination, children actually have an easier time catching balls that are thrown at a faster speed.

Which one of the following, if true, most helps to explain why very young children find it easier to catch balls that are thrown at a faster speed?

(A) Balls thrown at a faster speed, unlike balls thrown at a slower speed, trigger regions in the brain that control the tracking of objects for self-defense.

(B) Balls that are tossed more slowly tend to have a higher arc that makes it less likely that the ball will be obscured by the body of the adult tossing it.

(C) Adults generally find it easier to catch balls that are thrown slowly than balls that are thrown at a faster speed.

(D) Children are able to toss balls back to the adults with more accuracy when they throw fast than when they throw the ball back more slowly.

(E) There is a limit to how fast the balls can be tossed to the children before the children start to have more difficulty in catching them.

13. Like a genetic profile, a functional magnetic-resonance image (fMRI) of the brain can contain information that a patient wishes to keep private. An fMRI of a brain also contains enough information about a patient's skull to create a recognizable image of that patient's face. A genetic profile can be linked to a patient only by referring to labels or records.

The statements above, if true, most strongly support which one of the following?

(A) It is not important that medical providers apply labels to fMRIs of patients' brains.

(B) An fMRI has the potential to compromise patient privacy in circumstances in which a genetic profile would not.

(C) In most cases patients cannot be reasonably sure that the information in a genetic profile will be kept private.

(D) Most of the information contained in an fMRI of a person's brain is also contained in that person's genetic profile.

(E) Patients are more concerned about threats to privacy posed by fMRIs than they are about those posed by genetic profiles.

14. Council member: I recommend that the abandoned shoe factory be used as a municipal emergency shelter. Some council members assert that the courthouse would be a better shelter site, but they have provided no evidence of this. Thus, the shoe factory would be a better shelter site.

A questionable technique used in the council member's argument is that of

(A) asserting that a lack of evidence against a view is proof that the view is correct

(B) accepting a claim simply because advocates of an opposing claim have not adequately defended their view

(C) attacking the proponents of the courthouse rather than addressing their argument

(D) attempting to persuade its audience by appealing to their fear

(E) attacking an argument that is not held by any actual council member

15. It was misleading for James to tell the Core Curriculum Committee that the chair of the Anthropology Department had endorsed his proposal. The chair of the Anthropology Department had told James that his proposal had her endorsement, but only if the draft proposal she saw included all the recommendations James would ultimately make to the Core Curriculum Committee.

The argument relies on which one of the following assumptions?

(A) If the chair of the Anthropology Department did not endorse James's proposed recommendations, the Core Curriculum Committee would be unlikely to implement them.

(B) The chair of the Anthropology Department would have been opposed to any recommendations James proposed to the Core Curriculum Committee other than those she had seen.

(C) James thought that the Core Curriculum Committee would implement the proposed recommendations only if they believed that the recommendations had been endorsed by the chair of the Anthropology Department.

(D) James thought that the chair of the Anthropology Department would have endorsed all of the recommendations that he proposed to the Core Curriculum Committee.

(E) The draft proposal that the chair of the Anthropology Department had seen did not include all of the recommendations in James's proposal to the Core Curriculum Committee.

GO ON TO THE NEXT PAGE.

16. Travaillier Corporation has recently hired employees with experience in the bus tour industry, and its executives have also been negotiating with charter bus companies that subcontract with bus tour companies. But Travaillier has traditionally focused on serving consumers who travel primarily by air, and marketing surveys show that Travaillier's traditional consumers have not changed their vacation preferences. Therefore, Travaillier must be attempting to enlarge its consumer base by attracting new customers.

Which one of the following, if true, would most weaken the argument?

(A) In the past, Travaillier has found it very difficult to change its customers' vacation preferences.

(B) Several travel companies other than Travaillier have recently tried and failed to expand into the bus tour business.

(C) At least one of Travaillier's new employees not only has experience in the bus tour industry but has also designed air travel vacation packages.

(D) Some of Travaillier's competitors have increased profits by concentrating their attention on their customers who spend the most on vacations.

(E) The industry consultants employed by Travaillier typically recommend that companies expand by introducing their current customers to new products and services.

17. Educator: Traditional classroom education is ineffective because education in such an environment is not truly a social process and only social processes can develop students' insights. In the traditional classroom, the teacher acts from outside the group and interaction between teachers and students is rigid and artificial.

The educator's conclusion follows logically if which one of the following is assumed?

(A) Development of insight takes place only if genuine education also occurs.

(B) Classroom education is effective if the interaction between teachers and students is neither rigid nor artificial.

(C) All social processes involve interaction that is neither rigid nor artificial.

(D) Education is not effective unless it leads to the development of insight.

(E) The teacher does not act from outside the group in a nontraditional classroom.

18. The probability of avoiding heart disease is increased if one avoids fat in one's diet. Furthermore, one is less likely to eat fat if one avoids eating dairy foods. Thus the probability of maintaining good health is increased by avoiding dairy foods.

The reasoning in the argument is most vulnerable to criticism on which one of the following grounds?

(A) The argument ignores the possibility that, even though a practice may have potentially negative consequences, its elimination may also have negative consequences.

(B) The argument fails to consider the possibility that there are more ways than one of decreasing the risk of a certain type of occurrence.

(C) The argument presumes, without providing justification, that factors that carry increased risks of negative consequences ought to be eliminated.

(D) The argument fails to show that the evidence appealed to is relevant to the conclusion asserted.

(E) The argument fails to consider that what is probable will not necessarily occur.

19. Professor: One cannot frame an accurate conception of one's physical environment on the basis of a single momentary perception, since each such glimpse occurs from only one particular perspective. Similarly, any history book gives only a distorted view of the past, since it reflects the biases and prejudices of its author.

The professor's argument proceeds by

(A) attempting to show that one piece of reasoning is incorrect by comparing it with another, presumably flawed, piece of reasoning

(B) developing a case for one particular conclusion by arguing that if that conclusion were false, absurd consequences would follow

(C) making a case for the conclusion of one argument by showing that argument's resemblance to another, presumably cogent, argument

(D) arguing that because something has a certain group of characteristics, it must also have another, closely related, characteristic

(E) arguing that a type of human cognition is unreliable in one instance because it has been shown to be unreliable under similar circumstances

GO ON TO THE NEXT PAGE.

20. To date, most of the proposals that have been endorsed by the Citizens League have been passed by the city council. Thus, any future proposal that is endorsed by the Citizens League will probably be passed as well.

The pattern of reasoning in which one of the following arguments is most similar to that in the argument above?

(A)   Most of the Vasani grants that have been awarded in previous years have gone to academic biologists. Thus, if most of the Vasani grants awarded next year are awarded to academics, most of these will probably be biologists.

(B)   Most of the individual trees growing on the coastal islands in this area are deciduous. Therefore, most of the tree species on these islands are probably deciduous varieties.

(C)   Most of the editors who have worked for the local newspaper have not been sympathetic to local farmers. Thus, if the newspaper hires someone who is sympathetic to local farmers, they will probably not be hired as an editor.

(D)   Most of the entries that were received after the deadline for last year's photography contest were rejected by the judges' committee. Thus, the people whose entries were received after the deadline last year will probably send them in well before the deadline this year.

(E)   Most of the stone artifacts that have been found at the archaeological site have been domestic tools. Thus, if the next artifact found at the site is made of stone, it will probably be a domestic tool.

21. Chemist: The molecules of a certain weed-killer are always present in two forms, one the mirror image of the other. One form of the molecule kills weeds, while the other has no effect on them. As a result, the effectiveness of the weed-killer in a given situation is heavily influenced by which of the two forms is more concentrated in the soil, which in turn varies widely because local soil conditions will usually favor the breakdown of one form or the other. Thus, much of the data on the effects of this weed-killer are probably misleading.

Which one of the following, if true, most strengthens the chemist's argument?

(A)   In general, if the molecules of a weed-killer are always present in two forms, then it is likely that weeds are killed by one of those two forms but unaffected by the other.

(B)   Almost all of the data on the effects of the weed-killer are drawn from laboratory studies in which both forms of the weed-killer's molecules are equally concentrated in the soil and equally likely to break down in that soil.

(C)   Of the two forms of the weed-killer's molecules, the one that kills weeds is found in most local soil conditions to be the more concentrated form.

(D)   The data on the effects of the weed-killer are drawn from studies of the weed-killer under a variety of soil conditions similar to those in which the weed-killer is normally applied.

(E)   Data on the weed-killer's effects that rely solely on the examination of the effects of only one of the two forms of the weed-killer's molecules will almost certainly be misleading.

GO ON TO THE NEXT PAGE.

22. Principle: A police officer is eligible for a Mayor's Commendation if the officer has an exemplary record, but not otherwise; an officer eligible for the award who did something this year that exceeded what could be reasonably expected of a police officer should receive the award if the act saved someone's life.

Conclusion: Officer Franklin should receive a Mayor's Commendation but Officer Penn should not.

From which one of the following sets of facts can the conclusion be properly drawn using the principle?

(A) In saving a child from drowning this year, Franklin and Penn both risked their lives beyond what could be reasonably expected of a police officer. Franklin has an exemplary record but Penn does not.

(B) Both Franklin and Penn have exemplary records, and each officer saved a child from drowning earlier this year. However, in doing so, Franklin went beyond what could be reasonably expected of a police officer; Penn did not.

(C) Neither Franklin nor Penn has an exemplary record. But, in saving the life of an accident victim, Franklin went beyond what could be reasonably expected of a police officer. In the only case in which Penn saved someone's life this year, Penn was merely doing what could be reasonably expected of an officer under the circumstances.

(D) At least once this year, Franklin has saved a person's life in such a way as to exceed what could be reasonably expected of a police officer. Penn has not saved anyone's life this year.

(E) Both Franklin and Penn have exemplary records. On several occasions this year Franklin has saved people's lives, and on many occasions this year Franklin has exceeded what could be reasonably expected of a police officer. On no occasions this year has Penn saved a person's life or exceeded what could be reasonably expected of an officer.

23. Essayist: It is much less difficult to live an enjoyable life if one is able to make lifestyle choices that accord with one's personal beliefs and then see those choices accepted by others. It is possible for people to find this kind of acceptance by choosing friends and associates who share many of their personal beliefs. Thus, no one should be denied the freedom to choose the people with whom he or she will associate.

Which one of the following principles, if valid, most helps to justify the essayist's argument?

(A) No one should be denied the freedom to make lifestyle choices that accord with his or her personal beliefs.

(B) One should associate with at least some people who share many of one's personal beliefs.

(C) If having a given freedom could make it less difficult for someone to live an enjoyable life, then no one should be denied that freedom.

(D) No one whose enjoyment of life depends, at least in part, on friends and associates who share many of the same personal beliefs should be deliberately prevented from having such friends and associates.

(E) One may choose for oneself the people with whom one will associate, if doing so could make it easier to live an enjoyable life.

24. Physician: The rise in blood pressure that commonly accompanies aging often results from a calcium deficiency. This deficiency is frequently caused by a deficiency in the active form of vitamin D needed in order for the body to absorb calcium. Since the calcium in one glass of milk per day can easily make up for any underlying calcium deficiency, some older people can lower their blood pressure by drinking milk.

The physician's conclusion is properly drawn if which one of the following is assumed?

(A) There is in milk, in a form that older people can generally utilize, enough of the active form of vitamin D and any other substances needed in order for the body to absorb the calcium in that milk.

(B) Milk does not contain any substance that is likely to cause increased blood pressure in older people.

(C) Older people's drinking one glass of milk per day does not contribute to a deficiency in the active form of vitamin D needed in order for the body to absorb the calcium in that milk.

(D) People who consume high quantities of calcium together with the active form of vitamin D and any other substances needed in order for the body to absorb calcium have normal blood pressure.

(E) Anyone who has a deficiency in the active form of vitamin D also has a calcium deficiency.

GO ON TO THE NEXT PAGE.

25. Political philosopher: A just system of taxation would require each person's contribution to correspond directly to the amount the society as a whole contributes to serve that person's interests. For purposes of taxation, wealth is the most objective way to determine how well the society has served the interest of any individual. Therefore, each person should be taxed solely in proportion to her or his income.

The flawed reasoning in the political philosopher's argument is most similar to that in which one of the following?

(A) Cars should be taxed in proportion to the danger that they pose. The most reliable measure of this danger is the speed at which a car can travel. Therefore, cars should be taxed only in proportion to their ability to accelerate quickly.

(B) People should be granted autonomy in proportion to their maturity. A certain psychological test was designed to provide an objective measure of maturity. Therefore, those scoring above high school level on the test should be granted complete autonomy.

(C) Everyone should pay taxes solely in proportion to the benefits they receive from government. Many government programs provide subsidies for large corporations. Therefore, a just tax would require corporations to pay a greater share of their income in taxes than individual citizens pay.

(D) Individuals who confer large material benefits upon society should receive high incomes. Those with high incomes should pay correspondingly high taxes. Therefore, we as a society should place high taxes on activities that confer large benefits upon society.

(E) Justice requires that health care be given in proportion to each individual's need. Therefore, we need to ensure that the most seriously ill hospital patients are given the highest priority for receiving care.

26. A recent poll showed that almost half of the city's residents believe that Mayor Walker is guilty of ethics violations. Surprisingly, however, 52 percent of those surveyed judged Walker's performance as mayor to be good or excellent, which is no lower than it was before anyone accused him of ethics violations.

Which one of the following, if true, most helps to explain the surprising fact stated above?

(A) Almost all of the people who believe that Walker is guilty of ethics violations had thought, even before he was accused of those violations, that his performance as mayor was poor.

(B) In the time since Walker was accused of ethics violations, there has been an increase in the percentage of city residents who judge the performance of Walker's political opponents to be good or excellent.

(C) About a fifth of those polled did not know that Walker had been accused of ethics violations.

(D) Walker is currently up for reelection, and anticorruption groups in the city have expressed support for Walker's opponent.

(E) Walker has defended himself against the accusations by arguing that the alleged ethics violations were the result of honest mistakes by his staff members.

S T O P

IF YOU FINISH BEFORE TIME IS CALLED, YOU MAY CHECK YOUR WORK ON THIS SECTION ONLY.
DO NOT WORK ON ANY OTHER SECTION IN THE TEST.

SECTION IV

Time—35 minutes

27 Questions

<u>Directions:</u> Each set of questions in this section is based on a single passage or a pair of passages. The questions are to be answered on the basis of what is <u>stated</u> or <u>implied</u> in the passage or pair of passages. For some of the questions, more than one of the choices could conceivably answer the question. However, you are to choose the <u>best</u> answer; that is, the response that most accurately and completely answers the question, and blacken the corresponding space on your answer sheet.

In Alaska, tradition is a powerful legal concept, appearing in a wide variety of legal contexts relating to natural-resource and public-lands activities. Both state and federal laws in the United States assign
(5) privileges and exemptions to individuals engaged in "traditional" activities using otherwise off-limits land and resources. But in spite of its prevalence in statutory law, the term "tradition" is rarely defined. Instead, there seems to be a presumption that its
(10) meaning is obvious. Failure to define "tradition" clearly in written law has given rise to problematic and inconsistent legal results.

One of the most prevalent ideas associated with the term "tradition" in the law is that tradition is based
(15) on long-standing practice, where "long-standing" refers not only to the passage of time but also to the continuity and regularity of a practice. But two recent court cases involving indigenous use of sea otter pelts illustrate the problems that can arise in the application
(20) of this sense of "traditional."

The hunting of sea otters was initially prohibited by the Fur Seal Treaty of 1910. The Marine Mammal Protection Act (MMPA) of 1972 continued the prohibition, but it also included an Alaska Native
(25) exemption, which allowed takings of protected animals for use in creating authentic native articles by means of "traditional native handicrafts." The U.S. Fish and Wildlife Service (FWS) subsequently issued regulations defining authentic native articles as those
(30) "commonly produced" before 1972, when the MMPA took effect. Not covered by the exemption, according to the FWS, were items produced from sea otter pelts, because Alaska Natives had not produced such handicrafts "within living memory."
(35) In 1986, FWS agents seized articles of clothing made from sea otter pelts from Marina Katelnikoff, an Aleut. She sued, but the district court upheld the FWS regulations. Then in 1991 Katelnikoff joined a similar suit brought by Boyd Dickinson, a Tlingit from whom
(40) articles of clothing made from sea otter pelts had also been seized. After hearing testimony establishing that Alaska Natives had made many uses of sea otters before the occupation of the territory by Russia in the late 1700s, the court reconsidered what constituted a
(45) traditional item under the statute. The court now held that the FWS's regulations were based on a "strained interpretation" of the word "traditional," and that the reference to "living memory" imposed an excessively restrictive time frame. The court stated, "The fact that
(50) Alaskan natives were prevented, by circumstances beyond their control, from exercising a tradition for a

given period of time does not mean that it has been lost forever or that it has become any less a 'tradition.' It defies common sense to define 'traditional' in such
(55) a way that only those traditions that were exercised during a comparatively short period in history could qualify as 'traditional.'"

1. Which one of the following most accurately expresses the main point of the passage?

(A)   Two cases involving the use of sea otter pelts by Alaska Natives illustrate the difficulties surrounding the application of the legal concept of tradition in Alaska.

(B)   Two court decisions have challenged the notion that for an activity to be considered "traditional," it must be shown to be a long-standing activity that has been regularly and continually practiced.

(C)   Two court cases involving the use of sea otter pelts by Alaska Natives exemplify the wave of lawsuits that are now occurring in response to changes in natural-resource and public-lands regulations.

(D)   Definitions of certain legal terms long taken for granted are being reviewed in light of new evidence that has come from historical sources relating to Alaska Native culture.

(E)   Alaskan state laws and U.S. federal laws are being challenged by Alaska Natives because the laws are not sufficiently sensitive to indigenous peoples' concerns.

GO ON TO THE NEXT PAGE.

2. The court in the 1991 case referred to the FWS's interpretation of the term "traditional" as "strained" (line 46) because, in the court's view, the interpretation

(A) ignored the ways in which Alaska Natives have historically understood the term "traditional"
(B) was not consonant with any dictionary definition of "traditional"
(C) was inconsistent with what the term "traditional" is normally understood to mean
(D) led the FWS to use the word "traditional" to describe a practice that should not have been described as such
(E) failed to specify which handicrafts qualified to be designated as "traditional"

3. According to the passage, the court's decision in the 1991 case was based on which one of the following?

(A) a narrow interpretation of the term "long-standing"
(B) a common-sense interpretation of the phrase "within living memory"
(C) strict adherence to the intent of FWS regulations
(D) a new interpretation of the Fur Seal Treaty of 1910
(E) testimony establishing certain historical facts

4. The passage most strongly suggests that the court in the 1986 case believed that "traditional" should be defined in a way that

(A) reflects a compromise between the competing concerns surrounding the issue at hand
(B) emphasizes the continuity and regularity of practices to which the term is applied
(C) reflects the term's usage in everyday discourse
(D) encourages the term's application to recently developed, as well as age-old, activities
(E) reflects the concerns of the people engaging in what they consider to be traditional activities

5. Which one of the following is most strongly suggested by the passage?

(A) Between 1910 and 1972, Alaska Natives were prohibited from hunting sea otters.
(B) Traditional items made from sea otter pelts were specifically mentioned in the Alaska Native exemption of the MMPA.
(C) In the late 1700s, Russian hunters pressured the Russian government to bar Alaska Natives from hunting sea otters.
(D) By 1972, the sea otter population in Alaska had returned to the levels at which it had been prior to the late 1700s.
(E) Prior to the late 1700s, sea otters were the marine animal most often hunted by Alaska Natives.

6. The author's reference to the Fur Seal Treaty (line 22) primarily serves to

(A) establish the earliest point in time at which fur seals were considered to be on the brink of extinction
(B) indicate that several animals in addition to sea otters were covered by various regulatory exemptions issued over the years
(C) demonstrate that there is a well-known legal precedent for prohibiting the hunting of protected animals
(D) suggest that the sea otter population was imperiled by Russian seal hunters and not by Alaska Natives
(E) help explain the evolution of Alaska Natives' legal rights with respect to handicrafts defined as "traditional"

7. The ruling in the 1991 case would be most relevant as a precedent for deciding in a future case that which one of the following is a "traditional" Alaska Native handicraft?

(A) A handicraft no longer practiced but shown by archaeological evidence to have been common among indigenous peoples several millennia ago
(B) A handicraft that commonly involves taking the pelts of more than one species that has been designated as endangered
(C) A handicraft that was once common but was discontinued when herd animals necessary for its practice abandoned their local habitat due to industrial development
(D) A handicraft about which only a very few indigenous craftspeople were historically in possession of any knowledge
(E) A handicraft about which young Alaska Natives know little because, while it was once common, few elder Alaska Natives still practice it

GO ON TO THE NEXT PAGE.

The literary development of Kate Chopin, author of *The Awakening* (1899), took her through several phases of nineteenth-century women's fiction. Born in 1850, Chopin grew up with the sentimental novels that
(5) formed the bulk of the fiction of the mid–nineteenth century. In these works, authors employed elevated, romantic language to portray female characters whose sole concern was to establish their social positions through courtship and marriage. Later, when she
(10) started writing her own fiction, Chopin took as her models the works of a group of women writers known as the local colorists.

After 1865, what had traditionally been regarded as "women's culture" began to dissolve as women
(15) entered higher education, the professions, and the political world in greater numbers. The local colorists, who published stories about regional life in the 1870s and 1880s, were attracted to the new worlds opening up to women, and felt free to move within these worlds
(20) as artists. Like anthropologists, the local colorists observed culture and character with almost scientific detachment. However, as "women's culture" continued to disappear, the local colorists began to mourn its demise by investing its images with mythic significance.
(25) In their stories, the garden became a paradisal sanctuary; the house became an emblem of female nurturing; and the artifacts of domesticity became virtual totemic objects.

Unlike the local colorists, Chopin devoted herself
(30) to telling stories of loneliness, isolation, and frustration. But she used the conventions of the local colorists to solve a specific narrative problem: how to deal with extreme psychological states without resorting to the excesses of the sentimental novels she read as a youth.
(35) By reporting narrative events as if they were part of a region's "local color," Chopin could tell rather shocking or even melodramatic tales in an uninflected manner.

Chopin did not share the local colorists' growing nostalgia for the past, however, and by the 1890s she
(40) was looking beyond them to the more ambitious models offered by a movement known as the New Women. In the form as well as the content of their work, the New Women writers pursued freedom and innovation. They modified the form of the sentimental
(45) novel to make room for interludes of fantasy and parable, especially episodes in which women dream of an entirely different world than the one they inhabit. Instead of the crisply plotted short stories that had been the primary genre of the local colorists, the New
(50) Women writers experimented with impressionistic methods in an effort to explore hitherto unrecorded aspects of female consciousness. In *The Awakening*, Chopin embraced this impressionistic approach more fully to produce 39 numbered sections of uneven
(55) length unified less by their style or content than by their sustained focus on faithfully rendering the workings of the protagonist's mind.

8. Which one of the following statements most accurately summarizes the content of the passage?

(A) Although Chopin drew a great deal of the material for *The Awakening* from the concerns of the New Women, she adapted them, using the techniques of the local colorists, to recapture the atmosphere of the novels she had read in her youth.

(B) Avoiding the sentimental excesses of novels she read in her youth, and influenced first by the conventions of the local colorists and then by the innovative methods of the New Women, Chopin developed the literary style she used in *The Awakening*.

(C) With its stylistic shifts, variety of content, and attention to the internal psychology of its characters, Chopin's *The Awakening* was unlike any work of fiction written during the nineteenth century.

(D) In *The Awakening*, Chopin rebelled against the stylistic restraint of the local colorists, choosing instead to tell her story in elevated, romantic language that would more accurately convey her protagonist's loneliness and frustration.

(E) Because she felt a kinship with the subject matter but not the stylistic conventions of the local colorists, Chopin turned to the New Women as models for the style she was struggling to develop in *The Awakening*.

9. With which one of the following statements about the local colorists would Chopin have been most likely to agree?

(A) Their idealization of settings and objects formerly associated with "women's culture" was misguided.

(B) Their tendency to observe character dispassionately caused their fiction to have little emotional impact.

(C) Their chief contribution to literature lay in their status as inspiration for the New Women.

(D) Their focus on regional life prevented them from addressing the new realms opening up to women.

(E) Their conventions prevented them from portraying extreme psychological states with scientific detachment.

GO ON TO THE NEXT PAGE.

10. According to the passage, which one of the following conventions did Chopin adopt from other nineteenth-century women writers?

   (A) elevated, romantic language
   (B) mythic images of "women's culture"
   (C) detached narrative stance
   (D) strong plot lines
   (E) lonely, isolated protagonists

11. As it is used by the author in line 14 of the passage, "women's culture" most probably refers to a culture that was expressed primarily through women's

   (A) domestic experiences
   (B) regional customs
   (C) artistic productions
   (D) educational achievements
   (E) political activities

12. The author of the passage describes the sentimental novels of the mid–nineteenth century in lines 3–9 primarily in order to

   (A) argue that Chopin's style represents an attempt to mimic these novels
   (B) explain why Chopin later rejected the work of the local colorists
   (C) establish the background against which Chopin's fiction developed
   (D) illustrate the excesses to which Chopin believed nostalgic tendencies would lead
   (E) prove that women's literature was already flourishing by the time Chopin began to write

13. The passage suggests that one of the differences between *The Awakening* and the work of the New Women was that *The Awakening*

   (A) attempted to explore aspects of female consciousness
   (B) described the dream world of female characters
   (C) employed impressionism more consistently throughout
   (D) relied more on fantasy to suggest psychological states
   (E) displayed greater unity of style and content

14. The primary purpose of the passage is to

   (A) educate readers of *The Awakening* about aspects of Chopin's life that are reflected in the novel
   (B) discuss the relationship between Chopin's artistic development and changes in nineteenth-century women's fiction
   (C) trace the evolution of nineteenth-century women's fiction using Chopin as a typical example
   (D) counter a claim that Chopin's fiction was influenced by external social circumstances
   (E) weigh the value of Chopin's novels and stories against those of other writers of her time

15. The work of the New Women, as it is characterized in the passage, gives the most support for which one of the following generalizations?

   (A) Works of fiction written in a passionate, engaged style are more apt to effect changes in social customs than are works written in a scientific, detached style.
   (B) Even writers who advocate social change can end up regretting the change once it has occurred.
   (C) Changes in social customs inevitably lead to changes in literary techniques as writers attempt to make sense of the new social realities.
   (D) Innovations in fictional technique grow out of writers' attempts to describe aspects of reality that have been neglected in previous works.
   (E) Writers can most accurately depict extreme psychological states by using an uninflected manner.

GO ON TO THE NEXT PAGE.

Until the 1950s, most scientists believed that the geology of the ocean floor had remained essentially unchanged for many millions of years. But this idea became insupportable as new discoveries were made.

(5) First, scientists noticed that the ocean floor exhibited odd magnetic variations. Though unexpected, this was not entirely surprising, because it was known that basalt—the volcanic rock making up much of the ocean floor—contains magnetite, a strongly magnetic

(10) mineral that was already known to locally distort compass readings on land. This distortion is due to the fact that although some basalt has so-called "normal" polarity—that is, the magnetite in it has the same polarity as the earth's present magnetic field—other

(15) basalt has reversed polarity, an alignment opposite that of the present field. This occurs because in magma (molten rock), grains of magnetite—behaving like little compass needles—align themselves with the earth's magnetic field, which has reversed at various

(20) times throughout history. When magma cools to form solid basalt, the alignment of the magnetite grains is "locked in," recording the earth's polarity at the time of cooling.

As more of the ocean floor was mapped, the

(25) magnetic variations revealed recognizable patterns, particularly in the area around the other great oceanic discovery of the 1950s: the global mid-ocean ridge, an immense submarine mountain range that winds its way around the earth much like the seams of a baseball.

(30) Alternating stripes of rock with differing polarities are laid out in rows on either side of the mid-ocean ridge: one stripe with normal polarity and the next with reversed polarity. Scientists theorized that mid-ocean ridges mark structurally weak zones where the ocean

(35) floor is being pulled apart along the ridge crest. New magma from deep within the earth rises easily through these weak zones and eventually erupts along the crest of the ridges to create new oceanic crust. Over millions of years, this process, called ocean floor spreading,

(40) built the mid-ocean ridge.

This theory was supported by several lines of evidence. First, at or near the ridge crest, the rocks are very young, and they become progressively older away from the crest. Further, the youngest rocks all

(45) have normal polarity. Finally, because geophysicists had already determined the ages of continental volcanic rocks and, by measuring the magnetic orientation of these same rocks, had assigned ages to the earth's recent magnetic reversals, they were able to compare

(50) these known ages of magnetic reversals with the ocean floor's magnetic striping pattern, enabling scientists to show that, if we assume that the ocean floor moved away from the spreading center at a rate of several centimeters per year, there is a remarkable correlation

(55) between the ages of the earth's magnetic reversals and the striping pattern.

16. Which one of the following most accurately expresses the main idea of the passage?

(A) In the 1950s, scientists refined their theories concerning the process by which the ocean floor was formed many millions of years ago.

(B) The discovery of basalt's magnetic properties in the 1950s led scientists to formulate a new theory to account for the magnetic striping on the ocean floor.

(C) In the 1950s, two significant discoveries led to the transformation of scientific views about the geology of the oceans.

(D) Local distortions to compass readings are caused, scientists have discovered, by magma that rises through weak zones in the ocean floor to create new oceanic crust.

(E) The discovery of the ocean floor's magnetic variations convinced scientists of the need to map the entire ocean floor, which in turn led to the discovery of the global mid-ocean ridge.

17. The author characterizes the correlation mentioned in the last sentence of the passage as "remarkable" in order to suggest that the correlation

(A) indicates that ocean floor spreading occurs at an extremely slow rate

(B) explains the existence of the global mid-ocean ridge

(C) demonstrates that the earth's magnetic field is considerably stronger than previously believed

(D) provides strong confirmation of the ocean floor spreading theory

(E) reveals that the earth's magnetic reversals have occurred at very regular intervals

18. According to the passage, which one of the following is true of magnetite grains?

(A) In the youngest basalt, they are aligned with the earth's current polarity.

(B) In magma, most but not all of them align themselves with the earth's magnetic field.

(C) They are not found in other types of rock besides basalt.

(D) They are about the size of typical grains of sand.

(E) They are too small to be visible to the naked eye.

GO ON TO THE NEXT PAGE.

19. If the time intervals between the earth's magnetic field reversals fluctuate greatly, then, based on the passage, which one of the following is most likely to be true?

   (A)   Compass readings are most likely to be distorted near the peaks of the mid-ocean ridge.

   (B)   It is this fluctuation that causes the ridge to wind around the earth like the seams on a baseball.

   (C)   Some of the magnetic stripes of basalt on the ocean floor are much wider than others.

   (D)   Continental rock is a more reliable indicator of the earth's magnetic field reversals than is oceanic rock.

   (E)   Within any given magnetic stripe on the ocean floor, the age of the basalt does not vary.

20. Which one of the following would, if true, most help to support the ocean floor spreading theory?

   (A)   There are types of rock other than basalt that are known to distort compass readings.

   (B)   The ages of the earth's magnetic reversals have been verified by means other than examining magnetite grains in rock.

   (C)   Pieces of basalt similar to the type found on the mid-ocean ridge have been found on the continents.

   (D)   Along its length, the peak of the mid-ocean ridge varies greatly in height above the ocean floor.

   (E)   Basalt is the only type of volcanic rock found in portions of the ocean floor nearest to the continents.

21. Which one of the following is most strongly supported by the passage?

   (A)   Submarine basalt found near the continents is likely to be some of the oldest rock on the ocean floor.

   (B)   The older a sample of basalt is, the more times it has reversed its polarity.

   (C)   Compass readings are more likely to become distorted at sea than on land.

   (D)   The magnetic fields surrounding magnetite grains gradually weaken over millions of years on the ocean floor.

   (E)   Any rock that exhibits present-day magnetic polarity was formed after the latest reversal of the earth's magnetic field.

GO ON TO THE NEXT PAGE.

Passage A

Central to the historian's profession and scholarship has been the ideal of objectivity. The assumptions upon which this ideal rests include a commitment to the reality of the past, a sharp separation
(5) between fact and value, and above all, a distinction between history and fiction.

According to this ideal, historical facts are prior to and independent of interpretation: the value of an interpretation should be judged by how well it accounts
(10) for the facts; if an interpretation is contradicted by facts, it should be abandoned. The fact that successive generations of historians have ascribed different meanings to past events does not mean, as relativist historians claim, that the events themselves lack fixed
(15) or absolute meanings.

Objective historians see their role as that of a neutral judge, one who must never become an advocate or, worse, propagandist. Their conclusions should display the judicial qualities of balance and
(20) evenhandedness. As with the judiciary, these qualities require insulation from political considerations, and avoidance of partisanship or bias. Thus objective historians must purge themselves of external loyalties; their primary allegiance is to objective historical truth
(25) and to colleagues who share a commitment to its discovery.

Passage B

The very possibility of historical scholarship as an enterprise distinct from propaganda requires of its practitioners that self-discipline that enables them to
(30) do such things as abandon wishful thinking, assimilate bad news, and discard pleasing interpretations that fail elementary tests of evidence and logic.

Yet objectivity, for the historian, should not be confused with neutrality. Objectivity is perfectly
(35) compatible with strong political commitment. The objective thinker does not value detachment as an end in itself but only as an indispensable means of achieving deeper understanding. In historical scholarship, the ideal of objectivity is most compellingly embodied in
(40) the *powerful argument*—one that reveals by its every twist and turn its respectful appreciation of the alternative arguments it rejects. Such a text attains power precisely because its author has managed to suspend momentarily his or her own perceptions so as
(45) to anticipate and take into account objections and alternative constructions—not those of straw men, but those that truly issue from the rival's position, understood as sensitively and stated as eloquently as the rival could desire. To mount a telling attack on a
(50) position, one must first inhabit it. Those so habituated to their customary intellectual abode that they cannot even explore others can never be persuasive to anyone but fellow habitués.

Such arguments are often more faithful to the
(55) complexity of historical interpretation—more faithful even to the irreducible plurality of human perspectives— than texts that abjure position-taking altogether. The powerful argument is the highest fruit of the kind of thinking I would call objective, and in it neutrality

(60) plays no part. Authentic objectivity bears no resemblance to the television newscaster's mechanical gesture of allocating the same number of seconds to both sides of a question, editorially splitting the difference between them, irrespective of their perceived merits.

22. Both passages are concerned with answering which one of the following questions?

(A) What are the most serious flaws found in recent historical scholarship?

(B) What must historians do in order to avoid bias in their scholarship?

(C) How did the ideal of objectivity first develop?

(D) Is the scholarship produced by relativist historians sound?

(E) Why do the prevailing interpretations of past events change from one era to the next?

23. Both passages identify which one of the following as a requirement for historical research?

(A) the historian's willingness to borrow methods of analysis from other disciplines when evaluating evidence

(B) the historian's willingness to employ methodologies favored by proponents of competing views when evaluating evidence

(C) the historian's willingness to relinquish favored interpretations in light of the discovery of facts inconsistent with them

(D) the historian's willingness to answer in detail all possible objections that might be made against his or her interpretation

(E) the historian's willingness to accord respectful consideration to rival interpretations

GO ON TO THE NEXT PAGE.

24. The author of passage B and the kind of objective historian described in passage A would be most likely to disagree over whether

    (A) detachment aids the historian in achieving an objective view of past events
    (B) an objective historical account can include a strong political commitment
    (C) historians today are less objective than they were previously
    (D) propaganda is an essential tool of historical scholarship
    (E) historians of different eras have arrived at differing interpretations of the same historical events

25. Which one of the following most accurately describes an attitude toward objectivity present in each passage?

    (A) Objectivity is a goal that few historians can claim to achieve.
    (B) Objectivity is essential to the practice of historical scholarship.
    (C) Objectivity cannot be achieved unless historians set aside political allegiances.
    (D) Historians are not good judges of their own objectivity.
    (E) Historians who value objectivity are becoming less common.

26. Both passages mention propaganda primarily in order to

    (A) refute a claim made by proponents of a rival approach to historical scholarship
    (B) suggest that scholars in fields other than history tend to be more biased than historians
    (C) point to a type of scholarship that has recently been discredited
    (D) identify one extreme to which historians may tend
    (E) draw contrasts with other kinds of persuasive writing

27. The argument described in passage A and the argument made by the author of passage B are both advanced by

    (A) citing historical scholarship that fails to achieve objectivity
    (B) showing how certain recent developments in historical scholarship have undermined the credibility of the profession
    (C) summarizing opposing arguments in order to point out their flaws
    (D) suggesting that historians should adopt standards used by professionals in certain other fields
    (E) identifying what are seen as obstacles to achieving objectivity

S T O P

IF YOU FINISH BEFORE TIME IS CALLED, YOU MAY CHECK YOUR WORK ON THIS SECTION ONLY.
DO NOT WORK ON ANY OTHER SECTION IN THE TEST.

Acknowledgment is made to the following sources from which material has been adapted for use in this test booklet:

W. Jacquelyne Kious and Robert I. Tilling, *This Dynamic Earth: The Story of Plate Tectonics.* ©1996 by the United States Geological Survey.

"Open Your Mind." ©2002 by The Economist Newspaper Limited.

Elaine Showalter, *Sister's Choice: Tradition and Change in American Women's Writing.* ©1991 by Elaine Showalter.

Jennifer L. Tomsen, "'Traditional' Resource Uses and Activities: Articulating Values and Examining Conflicts in Alaska." ©2002 by Alaska Law Review.

Wait for the supervisor's instructions before you open the page to the topic.
Please print and sign your name and write the date in the designated spaces below.
Time: 35 Minutes

General Directions

You will have 35 minutes in which to plan and write an essay on the topic inside. Read the topic and the accompanying directions carefully. You will probably find it best to spend a few minutes considering the topic and organizing your thoughts before you begin writing. In your essay, be sure to develop your ideas fully, leaving time, if possible, to review what you have written. **Do not write on a topic other than the one specified. Writing on a topic of your own choice is not acceptable.**

No special knowledge is required or expected for this writing exercise. Law schools are interested in the reasoning, clarity, organization, language usage, and writing mechanics displayed in your essay. How well you write is more important than how much you write.

Confine your essay to the blocked, lined area on the front and back of the separate Writing Sample Response Sheet. Only that area will be reproduced for law schools. Be sure that your writing is legible.

Both this topic sheet and your response sheet must be turned over to the testing staff before you leave the room.

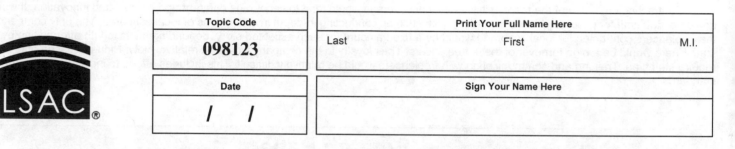

Topic Code	Print Your Full Name Here		
098123	Last	First	M.I.
Date	Sign Your Name Here		
/ /			

Scratch Paper
Do not write your essay in this space.

LSAT® Writing Sample Topic

> Directions: The scenario presented below describes two choices, either one of which can be supported on the basis of the information given. Your essay should consider both choices and argue for one over the other, based on the two specified criteria and the facts provided. There is no "right" or "wrong" choice: a reasonable argument can be made for either.

The biggest newspaper in a large market is deciding whether to continue to write all of its local stories in-house or to contract out much of this work off-site to local freelancers. The largest section of the newspaper is devoted to local coverage. Using the facts below, write an essay in which you argue for one choice over the other based on the following two criteria:

- The newspaper wants to maximize the quality of its local coverage.
- The newspaper wants to minimize the costs of producing local stories.

Writing all local stories in-house requires maintaining an extensive staff for this purpose. This involves expenditures for salaries, benefits, and overhead. Staff must also be reimbursed for employee business expenses associated with gathering stories. The day-to-day management of personnel frictions in a sizable staff can be challenging. Training and communicating with in-house staff is direct. This allows for the effective adoption and maintenance of strict standards. Different approaches and innovation tend to be discouraged.

Contracting out much of the responsibility for local coverage would tend to encourage different approaches and innovation. It would free up some staff time for potentially more rewarding work such as conducting in-depth investigations of local concerns. The only compensation for the freelancers contracted for local coverage would be a fixed amount for each accepted story, depending on its length after editing by in-house staff. There would be a high turnover of these freelancers. Their loyalty to the company would be relatively low. Hiring replacements would require staff time. Training and communicating with freelancers would be relatively difficult. This includes efforts to inculcate and enforce strict standards.

WP-S098A

Scratch Paper
Do not write your essay in this space.

COMPUTING YOUR SCORE

Directions:

1. Use the Answer Key on the next page to check your answers.

2. Use the Scoring Worksheet below to compute your raw score.

3. Use the Score Conversion Chart to convert your raw score into the 120–180 scale.

Scoring Worksheet

1. Enter the number of questions you answered correctly in each section.

	Number Correct
SECTION I.................	_____
SECTION II...............	_____
SECTION III..............	_____
SECTION IV	_____

2. Enter the sum here: _____
   This is your Raw Score.

Conversion Chart
For Converting Raw Score to the 120–180 LSAT Scaled Score
LSAT Form 2LSN93

Reported Score	Raw Score Lowest	Raw Score Highest
180	100	101
179	99	99
178	98	98
177	97	97
176	—*	—*
175	96	96
174	95	95
173	94	94
172	93	93
171	92	92
170	90	91
169	89	89
168	88	88
167	86	87
166	85	85
165	83	84
164	82	82
163	80	81
162	78	79
161	77	77
160	75	76
159	73	74
158	71	72
157	69	70
156	67	68
155	66	66
154	64	65
153	62	63
152	60	61
151	58	59
150	56	57
149	54	55
148	53	53
147	51	52
146	49	50
145	47	48
144	46	46
143	44	45
142	42	43
141	41	41
140	39	40
139	38	38
138	36	37
137	35	35
136	33	34
135	32	32
134	30	31
133	29	29
132	28	28
131	27	27
130	25	26
129	24	24
128	23	23
127	22	22
126	21	21
125	20	20
124	19	19
123	18	18
122	—*	—*
121	17	17
120	0	16

*There is no raw score that will produce this scaled score for this form.

ANSWER KEY

SECTION I

1.	C	8.	E	15.	C	22.	B
2.	B	9.	D	16.	D	23.	B
3.	C	10.	A	17.	C	24.	E
4.	D	11.	D	18.	E	25.	A
5.	B	12.	B	19.	C		
6.	A	13.	D	20.	B		
7.	B	14.	D	21.	E		

SECTION II

1.	E	8.	C	15.	A	22.	C
2.	B	9.	D	16.	B	23.	D
3.	A	10.	A	17.	B		
4.	C	11.	B	18.	B		
5.	E	12.	E	19.	C		
6.	B	13.	C	20.	E		
7.	D	14.	E	21.	A		

SECTION III

1.	E	8.	B	15.	E	22.	A
2.	D	9.	C	16.	E	23.	C
3.	E	10.	A	17.	D	24.	A
4.	A	11.	B	18.	A	25.	A
5.	D	12.	A	19.	C	26.	A
6.	D	13.	B	20.	E		
7.	B	14.	B	21.	B		

SECTION IV

1.	A	8.	B	15.	D	22.	B
2.	C	9.	A	16.	C	23.	C
3.	E	10.	C	17.	D	24.	B
4.	B	11.	A	18.	A	25.	B
5.	A	12.	C	19.	C	26.	D
6.	E	13.	C	20.	B	27.	E
7.	C	14.	B	21.	A